-0. MAY 1984

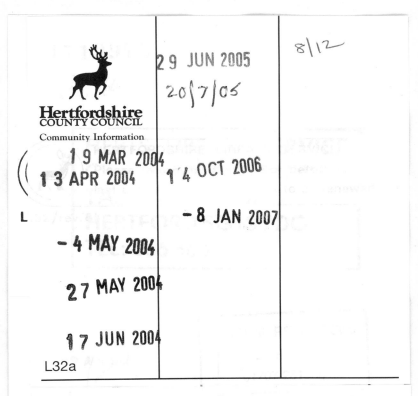

Hertfordshire
COUNTY COUNCIL
Community Information

29 JUN 2005

20/7/05

8/12

1 9 MAR 2004
1 3 APR 2004

1 4 OCT 2006

- 8 JAN 2007

L

- 4 MAY 2004

2 7 MAY 2004

1 7 JUN 2004

L32a

Please renew/return this item by the last date shown.

So that your telephone call is charged at local rate, please call the numbers as set out below:

	From Area codes 01923 or 0208:	From the rest of Herts:
Renewals:	01923 471373	
Enquiries:	01923 471333	
Minicom:	01923 471599	

L32b

D1349577

A B C OF TURF CULTURE

A B C

OF

TURF CULTURE

J. R. ESCRITT
Director, The Sports Turf Research Institute

KAYE & WARD
LONDON

ACKNOWLEDGEMENT

The author wishes to record his appreciation of the help given by all
Research Institute staff in compiling this volume and particularly to the
Assistant Director of the Institute, Mr. J. P. Shildrick.

HERTFORDSHIRE
LIBRARY SERVICE

635.964

1719975

First published in Great Britain by
Kaye & Ward Ltd,
21 New Street, London EC2M 4NT
1978

Copyright © Kaye & Ward Ltd. 1978

All rights reserved. No part of this publication may be reproduced,
stored in a retrieval system, or transmitted, in any form or by any means,
electronic, mechanical, photocopying, recording or otherwise, without
the prior permission of the copyright owner.   ·

ISBN 0 7182 1174 X

Photoset in VIP Palatino by S. G. Mason (Chester) Ltd.
Printed in Great Britain by Cox & Wyman Ltd.
London, Fakenham and Reading.

CONTENTS

INTRODUCTION

The quarterly twelve-page Sports Turf Bulletin issued to members by the Sports Turf Research Institute, aims to give them useful technical advice on the management of amenity turf areas. In addition to lawns, these include turf areas used for a great many outside sports – Association football, bowls, cricket, croquet, dog racing, golf, horse racing, lawn tennis, Rugby Union football, Rugby League football, school playing fields etc.

For all sports turf areas it is the quality of the playing surface which is important to the user and this very important point is seldom lost sight of in advice from the Sports Turf Research Institute. Repeated compliments on the helpfulness of the various articles in the Bulletin have prompted the production of this collection of recent articles (amended, up-dated and grouped as necessary) into book form so as to reach a wider readership than the Bulletin which is a 'members only' publication. The book deals in considerable detail with many subjects relevant to sports grounds, golf courses and various other turf areas but nevertheless gives a very comprehensive section on lawns – both making them and looking after them – for the amateur.

Articles for the Sports Turf Bulletin are written by all members of the staff of the Sports Turf Research Institute and this results in some variations in style and method of presentation. In basing this book on Bulletin articles I have allowed some of these to persist in the belief that such variations increase the reader's interest and make for easier reading without boredom! Through trying to present each subject as a unit in itself which can be studied *as a unit* it has not proved possible to avoid some degree of repetition and overlapping but it is hoped that the reader will appreciate the increased clarification achieved.

There is a shortage of authoritative text books on sports turf culture and the presentation of key topics in simple alphabetical order should assist all interested in sports turf management and particularly the increasing numbers of greenkeepers and groundstaff who are concerned in educational schemes and with passing examinations. Modern turf management calls for a good deal of scientific knowledge and here the book should help. Scientific knowledge is, however, no substitute for organisational ability or for the practical skills in carrying out the necessary operations and the judgement of the timing of these in relation to site, season, weather and user requirements which are so essential to success. Nor can it replace the common sense, hard work and dedication which so many greenkeepers, groundsmen and other turf managers produce in such generous measure.

In assembling this volume and its illustrations I have tried to be commercially unbiased and have generalised as far as seemed reasonable. In the illustrations of equipment an attempt has been made (subject to availability of photographs) to show something from as many firms as feasible. It should be noted that no endorsement of named products is implied or intended. Neither is the omission of any similar products to be taken as express or implied criticism.

AERATION

What is Meant

All kinds of people connected with amenity turf use the term turf aeration and so presumably the term is well understood. On the other hand, to some degree it means different things to different people. It is a general term used to cover various operations that are carried out to improve turf (especially the playing quality) by physical methods of adjusting sub-surface conditions so as to ventilate the soil, to improve drainage and to encourage better root development.

The term is unfortunately sometimes used rather slackly to mean some form of scarification to deal with the situation created by over-production of fibre at the surface of fine turf.

The Problems

Amenity turf, more particularly of course, that used for sport, is subjected to various forms of compaction – by the players themselves, by equipment used in general maintenance, by rolling when the game requires it and, unfortunately, many new areas have compaction built in during construction, e.g. the top soil has not been adequately cultivated and prepared. Compaction of top soil pushes the soil crumbs closer together and deforms them (sometimes very severely) so reducing the channels between the crumbs which allow movement of water through the soil and ventilation (oxygen in, carbon dioxide out). Compaction also restricts root development through physical obstruction and through the production of unsatisfactory conditions for their growth. Since compaction is facilitated by wet conditions it is not surprising to find its detrimental effects most pronounced on winter pitches.

Under fine turf areas it is often possible to see a succession of thin layers of different top dressing materials applied over the years. This condition impedes moisture movement and root development so that 'aeration' is often advantageous. Also on fine turf an unacceptable excess of fibre (mat or thatch) formation often occurs. There would appear to be more than one reason for this but, clearly, conditions restricting growth to the surface are contributory factors.

How the Problems are Dealt with

During the construction of new turf areas it is important to make sure that adequate preparation is carried out with proper top soil and sub-soil cultivations. It is rather upsetting when new turf has to be hollow tine forked to relieve compaction! Often in such circumstances the best course is to start again anyway.

On existing turf areas it is advisable (1) to restrict to a minimum consistent with play requirements all procedures likely to cause compaction, e.g. the use of heavy equipment and, of course, rolling; (2) to select from the wide range of aeration equipment which is marketed the type, make, size etc. which seems most suitable for the particular area and conditions concerned (and the pocket) – and use it!

Equipment available

(a) Equipment which extracts cores of earth, i.e. that with circular hollow tines, open sided rectangular tines, or spoon tines. Such equipment leaves holes which afford ready access for air and water and sods taken up a few months after the operation will usually show how roots have proliferated down the holes. This kind of operation relieves compaction by allowing soil around the holes to expand. The job is typically done in the autumn. In some cases the holes may be filled in or partially filled in with material aimed at preserving some of the benefits, e.g. by brushing in a sandy material to preserve some of the drainage improvements conferred by the holes on heavy soil.

This kind of aeration has great advantages for all kinds of turf but there are some disadvantages:

(i) There are practical difficulties in hollow tining large areas of turf such as football pitches and collecting the cores. Even on

4

relatively small areas like golf greens or bowling greens, collecting the cores can be a laborious chore, although leaf sweepers or core collectors can be used to simplify the operation.

(ii)   If this kind of aeration is carried out too frequently it is possible to produce a very soft and easily worn surface, i.e. to reduce the playing quality. In practice it is found that hollow tine forking once every three years is sufficient for most fine turf even when heavily used, although there are odd occasions where annual treatment is required. It is usually considered unwise to carry out this kind of aeration on cricket tables at all because of the risk of producing an unsatisfactory playing surface.

(iii)   A good protection against weed invasion is a strong unbroken turf and the holes created do facilitate weed invasion. This is one reason for avoiding excessive aeration of this type – on trial areas a pure weed-free bent sward has been known to become almost solid pearlwort after hollow tine forking in the autumn for three successive years.

Circular hollow tining has been used in this country for a very long time and because it leaves a clean hole is still very popular. It was first introduced through hand tools and for many people this is still the best equipment in that one can ensure 100 mm (4 in)

Hand hollow tine forking.

deep holes at regular intervals on every part of the area concerned. Nowadays, however, most hollow tining is done by mechanical equipment (self-propelled or tractor-drawn) and, of course, the same applies to the other methods of extracting soil.

(b)   Equipment with solid or slit tines. Hand equipment is available but, again, the job is more frequently carried out by machine. There are no doubt some differences between the effects of solid and slit tining but these differences are small compared with the difference of either from the effects of hollow tining. Solid and slit tines simply force holes into the soil and in so doing themselves create some degree of compaction. On the other hand, they do facilitate movement of water away from the immediate surface and allow some exchange of air. Their effects are much less than those of hollow tines and, to compensate, this kind of tining is carried out much more frequently. For heavily used winter pitches weekly solid or slit tining throughout the autumn to spring period is often beneficial and here a self-propelled machine is particularly valuable. On ill-drained fine turf frequent tining of this kind in the same season can be useful. Benefits from solid or slit tining in the summer are perhaps not so marked but penetration of rain or applied water is assisted by shallow spiking and, of course, this in turn means that fertilizers can be washed away from the surface a little better.

(c)   The Sub-air machine. This is a fairly recent introduction to this country so that it is perhaps too soon to attempt to assess its relative value. On the other hand, the nature of the machine suggests it should be very useful and opinions of the first users are generally favourable. In design the machine resembles a miniature sub-soil cultivator to which has been added a vibratory action. It will work down to 175 mm (7 in) and in use it leaves a clean cut with little surface disturbance unless there is very severe compaction or large stones.

(d)   The Turfquaker. With this machine off-set revolving blades cut a series of neat parallel slits about 50 mm (2 in) apart and 50–75 mm (2–3 in) deep, and cast a little fine earth onto the surface. Since the machine has not been around very long assessment of its usefulness is not easy but again there are some favourable reports.

6

Root development down holes made with hollow tine fork.

Some aerating machines arranged to show their working parts.

ALGAE

Both green algae and blue-green algae can be found in turf. They vary in appearance from a green slime to an almost black jelly-like material. They are usually a problem in turf only when there is bare ground for them to occupy and when the surface conditions are moist. Their presence thus indicates that some management treatment is necessary (especially drainage improvement). Creating conditions suitable for healthy and vigorous growth of the grass should be a sufficient approach but where it seems necessary (under trees for example) a possible control measure is the application of a copper sulphate solution containing 35 g/136 litre to an area of 100 m² (1 oz./25 gal. to 100 sq .yd.). Alternatively sulphate of iron could be used, 50 g/8 litre to 4 m² (1½ oz./1½ gal to 4 sq yd).

N.B. Excess of either chemical should be avoided — copper sulphate is well known as a plant poison.

ANNUAL MEADOW – GRASS *(Poa annua)*

This ubiquitous grass is one that is the subject of a great deal of discussion and argument. Most turf of whatever kind in the U.K. contains at least a little annual meadow-grass and many areas contain a good deal – even approaching a hundred per cent. It can be quite hard wearing and yet in most circles it is regarded as a weed grass, absence of which would be an advantage.

The species *Poa annua* has numerous ecotypes or possibly subspecies and, in the British Isles, a whole range of these can be found in turf. At one end of the range there is a type with large, broad leaves and an untidy, straggly and open growth habit, which may spread extensively by prostrate stems which root at the nodes; this type is prevalent under lenient mowing and use. At the other extreme there is a small-leaved type which forms low dense intermingling rosettes and which persists very well under close mowing and/or heavy wear.

8

Despite the name *annual* meadow-grass it is very questionable as to how much (if any) of this grass found in turf is a true annual. Certainly most of it is at least a short lived perennial and indeed a great deal of it behaves as a long lived perennial. The variation in types probably makes some contribution to the different opinions held about this grass.

On footpaths, under trees, on trodden roadside verges and the central area of roundabouts it may be the only grass which will survive. Indeed, because of the annual habit of some types, it has sometimes been sown on areas subject to heavy traffic fumes so that new self-sown plants can keep replacing dying plants. Such seed of annual meadow-grass as is commercially available is likely to approximate to a true annual, being cleanings from other seed crops.

Those with heavily used winter pitches frequently find that the predominant grass at the end of the playing season is annual meadow-grass. Since any grass is better than no grass at all this may be considered an advantage. On the other hand, despite renovation with seed of other grasses, during the summer it tends (especially on the wings of soccer pitches) to form a very thick spongy, fibrous turf which holds water in wet weather and kicks out in very large pieces during play.

In fine turf it is usually not very highly regarded though its elimination would leave a lot of bare ground in many cases. It is not a very fine grass compared with fine fescue and bent and its colour is not of the best. More important are its susceptibility to fusarium patch disease and to damage from drought or from hard weather in the winter when its colour is often noticeably poor. Its growth rate varies from that of other fine turf grasses and this sometimes leads to an untidy appearance. The prolific seed head production in early summer (the main period for it) gives an untidy, stubbly appearance and very much affects the quality of the playing surface. It does, however, flower throughout the year and its seeding capacity obviously contributes to the widespread existence of the grass – it rapidly seeds into bare patches!

For the many who wish to control annual meadow-grass science has not yet produced the full answer. When establishing new turf, particularly fine turf, thorough cleaning of the seed bed by fallowing or sterilisation ensures a complete cover of the sown grasses and this is turn helps to prevent invasion by annual meadow-grass. Good turf management can do much to keep it out but invariably it does invade sooner or later. There are now chemicals available which are of some value in preventing establishment of adventitious annual meadow-grass seed but they have so far been disappointing under British conditions. At present there are no known herbicides capable of selectively eliminating the grass from an established sward.

BOWLING GREENS

The Playing Surface

For the flat game it is essential that the surface should be flat, uniform, fast* and true. Crown bowlers seem to like a more 'interesting' surface which may have some undulations as well as the crown but the surface should also be fast and predictable. In both cases playing conditions are regarded as more important than appearance!

Autumn

As with all summer games autumn is a very important season and the time available to do the necessary work is all too short – extending the playing season creates problems in achieving satisfactory results from renovation and other work.

Fertilizer (see FERTILIZERS) treatment is a somewhat contentious subject. Many bowling greenkeepers give some form of special autumn or autumn/winter fertilizer treatment, (a complete fertilizer relatively low in nitrogen), but others time their last summer treatment for about the end of August and then give no more until the spring. The latter is preferable for many greens but possibly the former is more appropriate in some cases.

---

*The speed of a flat bowling green is measured as the number of seconds taken by a bowl from the time of its delivery to the moment it comes to rest, approximately 27.4 m (30 yd) from the mat line. On a slow green the time may be 10 seconds while on a good fast green the time might be 15 seconds. 20 seconds is a time which is probably only achieved in the U.K. in hot dry summers like 1976. N.B. Though puzzling the above figures are correct – there is no misprint!

A new works bowling green.

The main attack on straggly, procumbent growth and excessive surface fibre is made in early autumn before growth ceases. The manually operated wire rakes of yester-year have largely been superseded by powered equipment which means that surface scarification can be carried out the more quickly and thoroughly. A very thorough job can be done in the early autumn since any surface damage has time to recover before the next bowling season.

Whether worn areas are renovated by seed or by turf first-class work is required to ensure a really good surface finish. Grass seed (see GRASSES) should be sown just as soon after a green is closed as possible (preferably by mid-September and certainly not later than the end of September even in the South) but turfing can be done later in the autumn. Thorough preparation of the site is necessary in either case and a straight edge should be used to check levels.

To relieve compaction caused by play, the passage of mowers etc. so as to facilitate movement of air and water into the soil and to encourage rooting some form of aeration is usually necessary. Solid or slit tine work is often satisfactory but where compaction is severe removal of cores by hollow or spoon tines does a better job. The latter types of tining have disadvantages as well as advantages and are not normally necessary more frequently than at three year intervals.

Careful top dressing (usually with sandy compost material) is important to produce and maintain a smooth playing surface. In the early autumn this may be fairly heavy – 2 tonnes (2 tons) or more per full sized bowling green. Careful spreading and thorough working in is essential – with a drag brush or drag mat on a crown green, with a drag brush and/or a screed on a flat green.

Occasional topping with the mower should continue as long as there is grass growth, the height of cut being raised to 8 mm (5/16 in).

Winter

The green should be kept under constant observation so that any trouble can be dealt with immediately. Leaves should be swept off to avoid accumulations which could lead to disease and, in fact, this should be watched for in any case so that prompt treatment can be assured. Occasional topping with the mower may be required if the weather is mild.

Spring

When ground conditions permit careful light rolling preferably with a special bowling green roller should be carried out to correct any winter upheaval. A light top dressing of sandy compost is often beneficial.

As soon as suitable weather conditions prevail the spring fertilizer should be applied; this is usually a balanced complete fertilizer in powdered form (see FERTILIZERS) and accurate distribution (preferably with the assistance of a bulky carrier such as sandy compost) is very important. Proprietary mixtures are commonly used for convenience but the enthusiast makes up his own.

Thorough but gentle scarification is usually beneficial when there is sufficient steady growth. The first cuts should not be too severe, being no lower than 8 mm (5/16 in), the grass being taken down gradually to its summer height of 3–5 mm (2/16–3/16 in).

Summer

Mowing is clearly the most important and the most time consuming summer operation. During the playing season mowing should be frequent – as often as three times a week or more when the grass is growing vigorously – but not too severe since no grass thrives when cut at less than 3–5 mm (2/16–3/16 in). Cuttings should be boxed off. Heavy mowers should not be used on a bowling green but a very good quality mower is required – say one with ten or twelve blades to the cutting cylinder and giving a minimum of 110 cuts/metre (100 cuts per yard). When preparing for important matches the green should be mown diagonally, then brushed before mowing again on the opposite diagonal.

Occasional light rolling is usually desired but rolling should be kept to the minimum consistent with requirements.

Regular but very light scarification treatment eliminates procumbent growth.

Occasional slit or solid tining is beneficial.

Judgement is required to maintain sufficient growth without excess. Occasional light applications of a mainly nitrogenous fertilizer are usually considered worth while during the growing season and it is considered important to give a good dressing of fertilizer (mainly nitrogenous) towards the end of the growing season (say late August) to encourage growth in the autumn months which will help restore the turf after the wear and tear of the playing season.

Spraying with selective weedkiller may be required and timing is very important to obtain maximum benefit with minimum interference with the game.

In dry weather wise use of an efficient watering system may become essential. Water should be applied in good time – before the soil has completely dried out and the grass has started to become sick.

'Boxing' turf.

Rink Management

On flat greens regular moving of the rinks is important. On really well managed greens movement of 300 to 600 mm (1 to 2 ft) is a daily task and, of course, rinks should also be organised so that over a season, there is a similar amount of play north/south as there is east/west.

Gutters and Banks etc.

Maintenance of these in a clean and tidy state must be an integral part of the programme for bowling green management. On flat greens rink number plates, pegs used to hold rink marking lines etc. should have clean white paint.

It is also important for the pleasure of players that paths, flower beds and surrounding hedges should receive attention as appropriate.

Drag brush.

'BOXING' TURF

If turf available for laying is of uneven thickness it is wise to trim with the aid of a paring box. This consists of a shallow wooden tray of appropriate size with three sides which are of suitable size to provide the right thickness for the finished pieces of turf. The sides may have their outer edges protected by means of a metal strip. The turf is placed, grass side down, in the tray; fibre and soil on the other side are then removed down to the sides of the tray by planing them off with a scythe blade or a large two handled knife.

BRUSHING

Brushing may be done as a regular, routine operation on fine turf to perform a fairly gentle, but very useful, type of scarifying. It involves drawing a special wide stiff brush (a drag brush – not

15

an ordinary broom) smoothly over the surface. This raises stolons and other procumbent growth so that they can be mowed off and it helps to control the nap or grain which develops on some kinds of fine turf and which can affect the running of a ball. Brushing is also used to remove dew from the foliage and to smooth out top dressings and work them into the sole of the turf.

General turf areas also benefit from timely and judicious brushing to help smooth the surface during the winter and to get out dead material in the spring.

CAMOMILE (*Chamomile*)

Camomile *(Chamaemelum nobile)* is a non-grass plant which has found some favour for lawns since the middle ages. There are quite large areas of it in the lawns at Buckingham Palace and commercial material is advertised from time to time. Propagation is usually vegetative – shoots of a split up turf planted an inch or so apart grow together to form a sward. Camomile does not like acid conditions or very close mowing and it is difficult to keep a pure sward since grasses and weeds invade so readily.

CONSTRUCTION OF NEW SPORTS TURF AREAS

(See also ESTABLISHMENT)

Difficult maintenance problems, particularly bad drainage, on sports turf areas can often be traced back to inefficient construction in the first place. The work is usually done by contractors and the key points to watch are as follows:

Basic Information

It is most important, especially if the work is to be carried out by contract, to prepare accurate survey plans showing site boundaries, all physical features, i.e. hedges, old buildings, underground supply lines, etc., existing and new levels together with

Complete reconstruction of a League football ground.

the proposed layout. Test holes should be dug to ascertain the
depth and quality of the top soil and to find out the nature of the
sub-soil. On areas which require major grading the holes should
be at least 600 mm (2 ft) deeper than the final level proposed on
the cut side to ascertain sub-soil conditions at the depth drains
will be installed.

The layout of sports grounds should take into account the
preferred orientation for pitches (approximately north to south)
as well as the desirability of having any necessary slopes across
the line of play rather than with it. It should provide pitches of
appropriate size with suitable clearances and with allowance for
the effects of any banks which have to be constructed.

A golf architect is necessary to design a new golf course or
alterations to an existing one and frequently he organises all
specification documents.

Specification and Bills of Quantities etc.

If the work is to be carried out by contract, it is necessary to have a
precise specification (drawn up by a specialist) describing the

Tractor-mounted sub-soil cultivator.

work involved, how it is to be accomplished, the materials to be used and the sequence of operations. For most jobs it is advisable to prepare a Bill of Quantities in which all the work involved, together with all materials required, is accurately listed for the contractor to price. The preparation of a precise Specification and Bill of Quantities enables competitive tenders to be obtained. Work should be organised to take place during the drier summer months with sowing at the preferred time which is the end of the summer and turfing in the early autumn.

Grading

Only seldom is it practicable to adjust levels in the top soil satisfactorily. If it is necessary to alter considerably the contours of a site so as to produce the required levels it is vital that all the top soil is carefully stripped and stacked in convenient heaps prior to grading the sub-soil. Great care should be taken to prevent damage to top soil (or its contamination with sub-soil). To avoid future settlement the sub-soil filling should be laid in consecutive layers not exceeding 230 mm (9 in) in depth, each layer being adequately firmed. After smoothing off the sub-soil formation surface to the required even gradient top soil can be

18

re-spread to a uniform depth, preferably not less than 150 mm (6 in) firmed.

Sub-Soil Cultivation

After major grading works the sub-soil is severely compacted and water penetration impeded. To overcome this, it is necessary to 'shatter' the consolidated sub-soil by means of an operation known as sub-soil cultivation. (N.B. This is not mole ploughing.)

The operation should be carried out *after* top-soiling at intervals of 610 mm (2 ft) to a minimum depth of 460 mm (18 in) in a direction parallel to the line of the future main drains of the lateral system. Best results are obtained when the earth is dry and it is important that a sufficiently powerful tractor (preferably tracked) is used to pull the sub-soil cultivator to ensure smooth operation at a uniform depth.

Installing a Pipe-Drainage System

Practically all sports fields need pipe drains to remove excess water quickly and an expert is required to design the system and make sure it is properly installed (see DRAINAGE).

Tractor-towed sub-soil cultivator.

16531

Further Sub-Soil Cultivation

Drainage operations often cause further compaction of both top- and sub-soil. A second sub-soil cultivation is necessary to overcome this and also to provide channels along which water can flow to the drains. The operation is carried out as previously indicated, but amending the depth to clear the drains.

Cultivation, Soil Amelioration, etc. (see ESTABLISHMENT)

Special Turf Areas

Tennis courts, teeing grounds, bowling greens and golf greens demand special construction procedures.

Tennis courts and teeing grounds may be constructed entirely as above but with special care to detail or they may additionally have a complete 'drainage' layer of gravel or clinker ash.

Golf greens and bowling greens are usually (though not always) provided with a drainage layer and the 'soil' placed over this is a specially prepared mix containing a high proportion of sand and some peat. Details of the soil/sand/peat mix should be decided on the basis of laboratory hydraulic conductivity tests. In recent years a number of golf greens have been constructed without soil, grass being established in 250 to 300 mm (10 to 12 in) of suitable sand into the surface of which some peat has been mixed.

Some high quality winter pitches (e.g. for league soccer clubs) have been constructed on the lines of one or other of the two procedures outlined for golf greens.

Water Supply

During construction suitable arrangements should be made for providing a water supply to bowling greens, cricket tables, tennis courts, golf greens and at least those winter pitches which have a special construction involving a great deal of sand.

Further Reading

The book 'Sports Ground Construction — Specifications' by Gooch and Escritt and published jointly by the National Playing

Fields Association and The Sports Turf Research Institute provides very useful detailed information on the construction of new sports turf areas.

COTULA BOWLING GREENS

Cotula is a tiny low growing plant of the Composite family with small white flowers which is extensively used in preference to grass for bowling greens in New Zealand. *Cotula dioica* was the species originally used there but in recent years *Cotula maniototo* and *C. trailli:* ssp. *pulchella* have become increasingly popular. The plant first became the subject of publicity in Britain in 1974 as a result of the very favourable comments made by our Commonwealth Games Bowls Team who played on Cotula greens at Christchurch.

Advantages in New Zealand

Under conditions prevailing in New Zealand, Cotula has been found to have several advantages over normal turf. The plant is a small, creeping perennial herb which produces prostrate stems and stolons which root at intervals, thus providing a stable surface and a very uniform ground cover. It can be established quickly and recovers very rapidly if damaged by wear etc. Owing to its very low-growing habit it can be mown very closely without ill-effects, so providing an exceptionally fast bowling surface. It is not affected by heavy frosts or snow cover and hence has been found to provide a much longer playing season than grass greens in New Zealand. The speed of a Cotula green is said to be unaffected by wet weather and during the winter hardly any mowing or other maintenance is required.

Disadvantages in New Zealand

The New Zealanders' experience with Cotula bowling greens has suggested no overwhelming disadvantages. The plant does, however, take on a bronze colouration in winter – not a serious problem as far as bowling greens are concerned but a fact which seems to have limited its use for ornamental lawns in that country. In the North Island, where high summer temperatures and high humidity are encountered, the plant is very subject to fungal disease attack and damage by weevils. The present high cost of fungicides and insecticides may, therefore, force smaller clubs to return to grass greens in some areas. In the South Island, where climatic conditions more closely approximate to those found in Britain, disease causes few problems although insect pests remain troublesome.

One serious difficulty with a Cotula turf is, of course, weed control as most selective weedkillers can not be safely used on a sward where a non-grass species is the desirable plant. Over-all spraying with selective weedkillers can check the growth of the Cotula for up to two months so spot treatment of rosette-type weeds often has to be undertaken, MCPA or mecoprop being carefully applied to individual weeds by paint brush or small hand sprayer. For the control of grasses, all of which are weeds in this type of turf, reasonably effective results have been obtained using dalapon, but very careful application is required and some set-back of Cotula growth is unavoidable.

Establishment

Cotula is established not from seed but from plant fragments each usually consisting of a leaf and a piece of stem averaging about 25 mm (1 in) in length. These are obtained from established Cotula turf by special 'grooving' machines which are very severe scarifying machines. About 280 g of groovings, as the plant fragments are termed, are required to sow 1 m² (8 oz per sq yd). For a new green, groovings are evenly spread over a normally prepared bed and are then top dressed with a 3 mm (⅛ in) covering of screened soil. Regular watering is essential in dry weather and further light dressings of top soil are desirable during the variable establishment period.

Techniques have also been developed for establishing Cotula on existing grass greens, these involving equipment which makes a number of very small furrows or grooves at close intervals over the surface. Cotula groovings are then spread and raked into these furrows, the remaining grass being subsequently weakened by over-close cutting and herbicide treatment.

Cotula in Britain

Cotula dioica was introduced into this country many years ago as a rock garden plant but the plant has never been used here as a surface for sporting purposes. However, following the interest shown in the plant as a result of the Commonwealth Games, the Sports Turf Research Institute contacted the New Zealand Institute for Turf Culture and some 7·3 kg (16 lbs) of *Cotula pulchella* groovings were imported for study. These were 'sown' in June 1974 at the Institute's Experiment ground on an area of some 20 m² (24 sq yd). Good establishment was obtained but very regular hand weeding was found necessary to keep the plot free of annual meadow-grass and pearlwort. The Cotula developed a good ground cover in 1974 and retained it when cut at 3 mm (⅛ in) in spring 1975, but thinned out considerably later when subjected to even closer, i.e. very close, cutting. Weed invasion subsequently proved troublesome and the same poor winter colour was observed as in New Zealand. Progress in 1976 was not good and, on the advice of the English Bowling Association, further investigations were abandoned.

CRICKET

I. CRICKET TABLES

The Playing Surface

A cricket pitch needs to have a very special kind of surface. It must be really firm and true and the surface should hold together well and not break up during play. This means in practice that the surface soil needs to have a high proportion of clay to confer adhesion and that a considerable amount of rolling under the right moisture conditions is necessary to produce the 'solid' conditions required. Grass roots are important to help to reinforce the pitch but there must not be very much grass (in thickness or height) when the pitch is used.

Maintenance is an all-the-year-round operation although without a basically sound area of suitable turf growing in suitable soil with sufficient drainage it is very difficult indeed to produce good wickets.

The best time to start the year is the *end* of the cricket season. Immediately the cricket season ends the groundsman has to take all necessary steps to put things right ready for the next year.

Autumn

As with other areas of fine turf used for summer play, extending the growth into the autumn, within reason, is very useful. This is usually achieved by giving a suitable fertilizer dressing (see FER-TILIZERS) at the end of the summer (e.g. end of August) but groundsmen sometimes use in addition (or instead) a specially formulated autumn or autumn/winter fertilizer, which is usually a complete fertilizer relatively low in nitrogen.

When play ceases one of the first jobs is a thorough scarification to get out recumbent stems and debris and to ventilate the immediate surface. Wire rakes are often used but there's much to be said for mechanical scarifiers. Mowing may be required to clear up debris and long growth.

After scarification comes renovation with grass seed and clearly this must be sown as early as possible – preferably before the end of September. For general over-sowing or for thin areas within the body of the table a fine fescue/bent mixture (see GRASS-ES) is preferred but for thin areas at wicket ends and for bowlers' run ups coarser mixtures including a good cultivar of perennial ryegrass are often used. This is all right provided individual seeds of the coarser grasses are not allowed to blow into the square. For really badly worn areas turf is commonly used and accurate and careful work is necessary. The area to be turfed should be well prepared but left firm to receive the turf which should be laid accurately to the correct level using a wooden straight edge – trouble arises when the turf is laid 'proud' and obsti-nately refuses to settle down. Arrangements to get suitable turf should be made well ahead – a turf nursery is the best answer but unfortunately few clubs seem to be able to manage this.

24

After a season's rolling, penetration of air and moisture into the soil is restricted. The particles of soil are packed tightly together leaving precious little pore space. Even if one wanted to, one could not restore the soil to a 'natural' condition, but one can help air and water penetration by forking. Hollow tine forking is the best means of relieving compaction and letting in air and water but groundsmen report that this creates wickets which are unreliable and break up easily so hollow tining is practically never carried out on a cricket table. Solid tine forking is used instead and because of the solid nature of well prepared wickets 'hand' forking is often the only way to ensure sufficiently deep penetration – it is usual to aim at 100 mm (4 in) deep holes at 75–100 mm (3–4 in) centres. In view of labour shortage many people try and mechanise – often with unsatisfactory results. Restricting aeration to one spiking is not desirable and supplementary aeration at intervals is a good idea.

Top dressing with screened heavy loam or clay top soil is normally carried out after forking but it is important to press on with the work – top dressing should be done before growth ceases to reduce the risk of smothering and disease attack. The first purpose of the top dressing is to correct inequalities in the surface in the interests of play. It also makes for a smooth surface which when rolled will be uniformly compacted and which when mown will have a uniform amount of grass left. The amount to apply is a matter of skilled judgement – it may be anything from 0.5 to 2.5 kg/m^2 (1–5 lb per sq yd) and it should be thoroughly worked in by pulling a drag brush or working a lute several times in two directions. The screened soil should be in dry condition, applied to a dry surface and worked in while dry. To ensure this the soil should be obtained (on the basis of samples examined) well ahead so that when the season is finished the right material is there ready to use (protected from the weather of course).

Most people like to avoid having a lot of worms in the square, although a *few* worms in a square aren't necessarily a bad thing. The most commonly used material for earthworm control these days is chlordane applied as a proprietary product which may be solid or liquid, the latter being regarded as the most efficient. Early autumn – say October – is a good time to apply earthworm control material but suitable weather may also occur in the Spring.

Winter

The table is now ready to go through the winter but it should not be completely neglected. Occasional brushing may be required to further work in the top dressing or to disperse worm casts. Occasional switching to disperse dew should also be considered and mowing *may* be needed once or twice if there is mild weather. At the end of the playing season the mower should be raised to say 8 mm (5/16 in) and the grass maintained at this until good growth the following spring.

A close watch should be kept for disease, the main one of which is Fusarium patch disease which can cause severe damage if not tackled immediately by treating with a suitable fungicide – a treatment which may have to be repeated more than once – although serious trouble with disease is usually only encountered when maintenance is not of the best, e.g. too much of the wrong fertilizer at the wrong time.

During the autumn and winter months there may be time available to hand weed out coarse grass patches which show up more clearly when the grass has on its 'winter coat', i.e. it is a bit longer than during the season. Odd daisies etc. may be removed at the same time.

Spring

When spring weather appears near, the first careful light rolling is commenced to get a general firmness on which to produce individual wickets. As growth begins raking or mechanical scarification is carried out to get the turf to a suitable density – grass growth to produce good root is necessary but cricketers do not like a thick carpet of turf. Spring fertilizer is then applied – a complete dressing in proprietary form or one made up from the normal constituents of such mixtures:

> sulphate of ammonia
> dried blood and/or fine hoof and horn meal
> superphosphate
> fine bone meal
> sulphate of potash

A carrier of screened soil is recommended to facilitate even distribution and minimise scorch risk. Usually rain will wash in the fertilizer but if no rain comes in one or two days watering in may be necessary.

Early in the spring it is a mistake to cut the grass too short – 8 mm (5/16 in) is close enough until the weather allows reliable growth. After this it should be maintained at 5 mm (3/16 in) except in the preparation of individual wickets when the mower may be set to 2 mm (1/16 in) – provided that the surface is smooth enough.

When growth is really vigorous, say about a fortnight after the spring fertilizer, consideration should be given to selective weedkilling since weeds spoil playing properties as well as appearance. If weedkilling is necessary then a proprietary selective weedkiller should be applied at the maker's recommendations with a suitable sprayer on a dry day when the ground is sufficiently moist to encourage growth. Sometimes a second spray may be necessary, say after 3–4 weeks. *Do not try* to ensure 100% weed elimination in one treatment by using more than the recommended rate of weedkiller since damage to grass may result.

Summer

During the playing season a main requirement is the regular and skilful use of the roller under the correct soil moisture conditions. Marking out is also a time consuming operation which is much assisted by permanent markers placed just below the surface to mark the four corners of the table plus side markers for the crease.

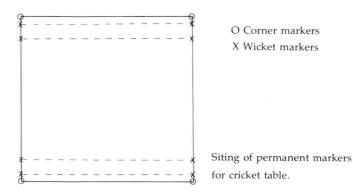

O Corner markers
X Wicket markers

Siting of permanent markers
for cricket table.

A drying roller sometimes used to remove surface water from cricket tables.

Scarification is required from time to time and, of course, mowing which is a very important operation that often fails to receive the attention it deserves. A mower in good condition is needed and it should be used *regularly,* preferably when the grass is not too long and when it is dry. Switching or brushing to disperse moisture in the morning may ensure a dry cut in the afternoon. Cuttings should be boxed off.

Occasional watering may be necessary and here again careful judgement is required. Before watering pricking the surface with a shallow pricking machine may be desirable to help the water in. A little fertilizer of a nitrogenous kind may be needed from time to time but the aim is not a lot of growth but a good cricket wicket. Nevertheless without some top growth it is impossible to get root growth and roots are the reinforcement in the rolled earth which forms the cricket surface. It is particularly important to ensure sufficient fertilizer at the end of the summer to keep a reasonable amount of growth during the early autumn months. Suitable fertilizer at about the end of August is usually satisfactory but sometimes an autumn or autumn/winter fertilizer may be used in addition (or instead).

The final preparation of a pitch for a match begins about ten days beforehand. The turf is mown very short, thoroughly scarified and again mown short. When a suitable thinness has been produced it is kept like that by repeated close mowing. Rolling the pitch under the right soil moisture conditions is also carefully carried out to produce the degree of solidity considered appropriate.

After each use urgent attention to restoration is important. The surface of the used pitch should be brushed and mown. If it is to be used again then temporary repairs are necessary including filling block holes and bowlers' footholes. When a pitch comes out of play for the season every effort should be made to complete renovation as soon as possible, thus giving it a full year to recover.

Renovation requires the scratching up of some kind of a seed bed. A useful method of getting seed established on patches which have lost their grass but maintained their levels involves the use of a special home-made rake. This is made from a short toothed (well worn) garden rake by filing the teeth into knife edges parallel to the handle. By means of this rake grooves can be made in the surface into which soil and seed can be rubbed.

II CRICKET OUTFIELDS

What is really the function of the outfield? Most people in cricket (though perhaps not the bowlers!) would agree that it is to act as a platform over which the ball may travel quickly from the cricket table in the direction of the boundary. The fielder requires a smooth true surface to the outfield so that he can pick up a swiftly moving ball with no fear that it will jump up and hit him in the face. With the objective of a good smooth fast true outfield the following programme of maintenance from autumn to autumn might be appropriate.

In autumn the table must have priority but there are one or two important jobs on the outfield which should be squeezed in as well if at all possible.

The first of these may be a really good scarifying in September or early October at the latest. A chain harrow or tractor-mounted rake will scarify the outfield efficiently and quickly. When there is plenty of time and the fibre mat at the surface is really thick the larger self-propelled vertical cutting machines have been used with good effect.

One of the best times to remove worms is in the autumn during mild wet weather when the worms are near the surface. Chlordane at present is one of the best wormkillers to use for clearing worms out of a cricket outfield.

The outfield should be well spiked through the autumn and early winter whenever soil conditions and time allow, paying particular attention to the path of the motor roller from the edge of the outfield to the table. Regular travel out to the square and back produces a really hard track and it is sometimes worth while using hollow tines where the soil is particularly hard.

Fine grasses which produce a fast true turf flourish in soils which are slightly acid. This is partly the reason why some of the best cricket outfields are to be found in industrial areas like south Yorkshire, Lancashire and north Cheshire. If the groundsman is not careful, however, the soil can easily become too acid and then there is trouble. A thick spongy mat of fibre develops and the turf becomes weak and full of moss. If lime is needed to correct over-acidity then autumn or winter is the time to get it on. Where lime deficiency is suspected it is wise to send a fully representative soil sample from the outfield for chemical analysis in a reputable laboratory and ask for advice on how much lime to give.

Sometimes a cricket club will allow a hockey club to use the ground during the winter, or a cricket and hockey club may share the same ground. The ideal is to have no winter games on a cricket outfield but if it is a case of 'doubling-up' like this then hockey is really the only safe companion game for cricket. Soccer and Rugby must quite often be played on cricket outfields in the case of general sports clubs and schools but the outfields rarely survive unscathed the rigours of the football season. Moreover although the tables themselves may be fenced off players in the winter may still damage the turf on them when jumping over the fences to retrieve their footballs.

Spring

In late February or early March the outfield should receive a light scarifying and then a good spiking. The scarifying will tear out the dead growth which has accumulated during the winter and the spiking will let more air into the soil so that the grass roots can go down deeper. A light rolling might be given in March if really needed but should be avoided unless the job is really necessary. The cricket table roller will probably be too heavy for overall use on the outfield and a tractor drawn sports ground or wide farm roller will be better. One of the larger motor mowers may weigh between 150 kg and 300 kg (3 and 6 cwt) and therefore mowing the outfield with one of these involves quite a substantial amount of rolling each time so that additional rolling is seldom required.

Moss sometimes gets into an outfield especially if there are some higher spots which are skinned by the mower. A good time to treat the moss is on a fine day in February or March and a good mosskiller to use then is one of the mercurised moss dressings which contains also some quick acting nitrogen.

There is not always money available for a spring fertilizer – nor does the outfield necessarily need one every year. A lot depends on the inherent fertility of the soil. Some grounds will need an annual fertilizer each spring or every second spring; others will need a fertilizer only every four of five years perhaps. When the grass seems really weak in the spring and a fertilizer does seem necessary a good choice might be a balanced complete fertilizer to be applied evenly in showery weather during April, e.g. a granular containing 10% N, 15% P_2O_5 and 10% K_2O at 375 kg/ha (3 cwt per acre).

When the outfield has been used for winter games there will probably be at least some scars and holes which should be topped up level with light sandy top soil and oversown with a suitable seeds mixture (chosen to match existing turf) in early April (following the spring fertilizer treatment, if this is given). After football there may be need for considerable renovation!

31

If weeds develop these should be controlled by spraying with a suitable selective weedkiller during a spell of fine weather from April to September, preferably during the spring in the case of most weeds. Care is necessary to use the right sort of chemical at the correct rate, suitably diluted in water, and to apply the weed-killer evenly and accurately over the weedy turf.

Mowing the outfield should be done frequently and fairly closely but not too closely otherwise the turf will be weakened. During a dry summer the mower might be set a little higher than is normal. The best finish is obtained with a motor mower fitted with box for collecting the clippings but on the average sports ground and school playing field the cricket outfield is usually mown, for the sake of speed and convenience, like the rest of the ground, i.e. with a set of gang mowers. Even so, for an important cricket match when something of a show is wanted, it is worth while spending a little extra time and using a motor mower with box for cutting the outfield the day before the match.

CULTIVAR

Each of the common turfgrass species may exist in a number of varieties. A cultivar is a *culti*vated *vari*ety. Plant breeders are continuously trying to produce better cultivars. They, the sellers of new cultivars and the advertising agents, are prone to bias so that considerable care is required in choosing which cultivars to buy. For agriculture, cultivar testing by official bodies is compulsory but this is not so for turf culture. Nevertheless a good deal of information from independent tests is available in the reports of trials carried out by The Sports Turf Research Institute.

DIMENSIONS OF SPORTS AREAS

Unless otherwise indicated, equivalent metric measurements are those suggested by the governing body of the sport concerned.

ASSOCIATION FOOTBALL

Length	90 m to 120 m	(100 yd to 130 yd)
Width	45 m to 90 m	(50 yd to 100 yd)

BASKET BALL

Length	26 m (28 yd)
Width	14 m (15½ yd)

Variations of ± 2 m (2 yd) on length and ± 1 m (1 yd) on width are permitted

CRICKET PITCH

Length	20.12 m (22 yd)
Width	3.05 m (10 ft)

CROQUET LAWN

Full size	32 m × 25.5 m	(35 yd × 28 yd)

CROWN BOWLING GREEN – *Direct metric conversions.*

A square with side varying from 27.5 m to 55 m
(30 yd to 60 yd).
The crown is commonly 150 mm to 375 mm
(6 in to 15 in) depending on the size of the green

FLAT BOWLING GREEN

A square of side not less than 36.57 m (40 yd) and not more than 40.23 m (44 yd) not including ditch. Variations are possible e.g. a rectangular shape with longer side not more than 40.23 m (44 yd) and the shorter side not less than 30.17 m (33 yd).

HOCKEY

91.40 m × 55 m   (100 yd × 60 yd).

LACROSSE

MEN
Length, minimum 100 m (110 yd)
Width, maximum   64 m (70 yd)

WOMEN
Length, minimum 110 m (120 yd)
Width, minimum   75 m (85 yd)

LAWN TENNIS

Court Length   23.77 m (78 ft)

Width   Singles 8.23 m (27 ft) Doubles 10.97 m (36 ft)

Run back   general minimum 5.49 m (18 ft), international minimum 6.4 m (21 ft)

Space between courts   minimum 3.66 m (12 ft)
Space between courts and fence minimum 3.05 m (10 ft)

NETBALL

30.5 m × 15.25 m   (100 ft × 50 ft).

POLO – *Direct metric conversions*

Length   not more than 274.3 m (300 yd)
Width   not more than 182.8 m (146.3 m if boarded) (200 yd) (160 yd)

RUGBY FOOTBALL

Length   not exceeding 100 m (110 yd)
Width   not exceeding   69 m (75 yd) (68 m (75 yd) for Rugby League)

Depth in goal area at each end   Rugby Union, not exceeding 22 m (25 yd)
Depth in goal area at each end   Rugby League, 5.5 m – 11 m (6 yd – 12 yd)

ATHLETICS

Metric Tracks – two parallel lines joined at either end by a semi-circle according to the following measurements will give a 400 metre track measured 300 mm from the inside edge.

34

Lengths of Parallels – 84.39 m. Radius of Semi-circle – 36.50 m.

To give a track of 4 laps to the mile measured 1 ft from the inner edge of the track the following table of measurements can be used.

Length of Parallels	Radius of Semi-Circle
225 ft	137 ft 5½ in
240 ft	132 ft 8¼ in
*270 ft	123 ft 1⅝ in
300 ft	113 ft 7 in

*most suitable measurement

Conversion of existing tracks involves lifting the inner kerb at one end of the track and moving it inwards so as to shorten the track length appropriately. Any track of 440 yd can be converted to a 400 m track by reducing the length of each parallel by 3 ft 9⅛ in and adjusting the centre of the semi-circle, but not the radius, at one end accordingly. Conversion of new metric tracks to yard lengths involves temporary curves to extend the length.

Dimensions of Landing Areas

High Jump	5 m × 4 m (16 ft 4 in × 13 ft 1½ in)
Long Jump	9 m × 2.75 m (30 ft × 9 ft), Take off board minimum 1m (3 ft) in front of landing area
Triple Jump	7.3 m × 2.75 m (minimum) Take off board 11 m from landing area (24 ft × 9 ft) Take off board 36 ft from landing area
Pole Vault	5 m × 5 m (16 ft 4 in × 16 ft 4 in)

Dimensions of Run Ups

Long Jump	40 m – 45 m × 1.22 m (130 ft – 147 ft 6 in × 4 ft 3 in)
Triple Jump	40 m – 45 m × 1.22 m (130 ft – 147 ft 6 in × 4 ft 3 in)
Pole Vault	40 m – 45 m × 1.22 m (130 ft – 147 ft 6 in × 4 ft 3 in)
Javelin	30 m – 36.5 m × 4.27 m (98 ft 6 in — 119 ft 9 in × 14 ft)

Semi-circle with 15 m – 18 m (49 ft 3 in – 59 ft) radius.

TO CONSTRUCT A RIGHT ANGLE USING THE 3:4:5 METHOD

If three lengths of material are placed so that their ends just touch as in the diagram below, a right angle will be formed if the lengths used are 3, 4 and 5.

The unit of measurement can be anything convenient (e.g. metres, feet) as it is the proportions (3:4:5) that are important. It follows that any multiple of the units will also be suitable, e.g.

3:4:5
or 6:8:10
or 1½:2:2½ etc.

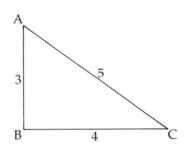

For small areas it can be useful to make a permanent triangle using wood for the three sides. A more portable instrument can be produced using wood for one side and cord for the others, so that when the cords are tight a right angle is formed.

A tape measure can be used for larger areas (because a larger triangle will produce a more accurate angle). The whole triangle can be made from the one tape.

If working single-handed, the first step is to find 12 units (or a suitable multiple) so that the three sides can be made (3 + 4 + 5 = 12).

The two ends (i.e. 0 and 12) are then pegged together thus fixing one corner (B). The tape is then stretched along the base line to the next corner (C) 4 units away from B, and a peg placed there to fix it.

Finally the right angle is established by tightening the loose sides of the triangle and placing the last peg at point A, 3 units from B (this should make the side AC 5 units in length).

The angle at B will then be 90°.

DISEASES OF TURF

I. WHAT IS MEANT BY DISEASE?

'Disease' is a word that most turf managers would think they understood but it proves very difficult to give a satisfactory definition. It has been said that disease is a departure from normal growth or function sufficient to cause either visible symptoms or loss of yield. This, however, merely shifts the difficulty into deciding what is 'normal' and how much 'departure' is permissible. The problem is that 'healthy' or 'diseased' are not two separate, distinct states, and it is not possible to distinguish a sharp transition between them. Of course, on some occasions, the deviations from normal health are so marked as to be unmistakable but this is not always the case.

Causes of Disease

(a) Environmental

Within the rather wide definition of disease suggested above, it could be said that many things can cause disease, e.g. various environmental factors can cause a lowering of growth rate and loss of colour. Perhaps one of the most common is low fertility, especially with regard to major nutrients such as nitrogen, but sometimes problems may occur due to lack of magnesium, iron or one of the many other elements required for normal growth.

Weather conditions may also play a significant part in affecting growth of the grasses, whether by drought during the summer or by frost during the winter.

(b) Biological

Organisms which attack living plants and cause disease are called pathogens, although some people use this word to cover non-living disease-causing factors as well.

It is perhaps appropriate to consider here why organisms have such a life-style. The green plant contains a complex mechanism by which it can carry out a process known as photosynthesis during which light energy falling on the plant is transformed into chemical energy. For an animal, like ourselves, food may be obtained directly by eating plants or indirectly by eating other animals which, themselves, have fed upon plants.

Fungi, although sometimes regarded as plants, do not have the mechanism for using sunlight as energy and are thus like animals in their dependence upon green plants. Some fungi obtain their food from dead plant or animal material. Such fungi are called saprophytes. They play an essential role in the break-down of dead material, releasing nutrients which can then be re-used by green plants.

Some of these fungi can attack living plants – indeed many of the most damaging diseases of turfgrasses are caused by such fungi. However, some other fungi do not behave in this way, being totally dependent on living plant material.

Plants can also be attacked by viruses which use the machinery of the plant cell to reproduce themselves. Infected plants sometimes have a mottled appearance but on other occasions there may be little outward sign of infection, thus making the presence of the virus difficult to detect. However, the growth of the plant may be affected and this could have a weakening effect. Virus diseases of turfgrasses are still little understood and require much further study.

(c) Interactions

So far the causes of disease have been described as if they occurred independently but nothing could be further from the truth. We should instead try to think of the turfgrass sward as being influenced by a large range of inter-acting factors. Among these factors are the species of grass and the particular cultivars, weeds, the weather, fertility, management practices, usage (e.g. wear), environmental pollutants, disease-causing organisms and animals. Many of the interactions between these factors are still very imperfectly understood. However, some associations between certain of them have been noticed, e.g. the relationship between lack of nitrogen and the obvious symptoms of corticium disease. Another example is the connection between weather conditions and the development of fusarium patch disease.

The effects of fungal disease may be dramatic in the short term, as is the case with fusarium patch disease which may cause the destruction of large areas of susceptible types of grass in a few days, or less obvious and therefore less well understood, e.g. with some of the fungi causing leaf spots.

In succeeding sections fungal diseases are dealt with quite fully but more comprehensive information is to be found in the book 'Fungal Diseases of Turf Grasses' published by The Sports Turf Research Institute.

II. FUNGICIDES IN TURF USE

It is important to remember that cultural practices have a large influence on fungal disease development and this aspect should at all times receive great attention. The use of the correct fertilizer and the timing of its application are particularly important in this respect. Unfortunately, although disease outbreaks can be reduced by proper management they are not entirely prevented and fungicidal treatment is sometimes necessary.

Except on areas which experience has shown to be particularly disease susceptible, curative treatment rather than preventive spraying is to be recommended. The reason for preferring curative to preventive treatment is that trials in the U.K. and in the U.S.A. have shown that preventive spraying can lead to an increase in disease after the effect of the treatment wears off. A further consideration is the cost in both money and time of such a programme. Curative treatment, if it is to be really effective, should be made as soon as possible after the onset of the disease and this makes necessary correct disease recognition and watchfulness on the part of the turf manager.

In the following sections various fungicides are referred to by their common name. Details of trade products containing particular fungicides can be obtained from the booklet 'Approved Products for Farmers and Growers' published by the Ministry of Agriculture as a part of the Agricultural Chemicals Approval Scheme. This booklet also gives information on insecticides and herbicides.

Fungicides containing Copper

Fungicides containing copper were among the first fungicidal materials to be used on sports turf. An example of such a material is Bordeaux mixture, which can be made by mixing in correct proportions a solution of copper sulphate with a suspension of hydrated lime but which is also available as a prepared powder to mix only with water. For turf use it is usual to add to ready prepared Bordeaux mixture a green dye, malachite green, which itself has some fungicidal effect and also acts as a marker. This material, i.e. Bordeaux mixture with malachite green, controls fusarium patch disease and corticium disease (red thread). It is very cheap for a single application but there are disadvantages. It is very messy and the persistence of the material is quite short – in rainy weather applications may have to be repeated every 7 days. Moreover, if the material is used regularly over a period of years there may be a build up of copper in the soil which can be detrimental to grass growth.

Another fungicide containing copper is Cheshunt compound. This material is useful on small areas for the control of diseases of seedlings.

Fungicides containing Mercury

There are two groups of these materials – those based on inorganic mercury and those based on organic mercury.

Inorganic Mercury Compounds

The two inorganic salts used are mercuric chloride (corrosive sublimate) and mercurous chloride (calomel). Most commercial fungicides of this type contain both salts. Sprayable and dry application formulations are available. Diseases controlled include fusarium patch disease, corticium disease and damping-off disease. These materials are very effective fungicides but are poisonous to man and also rather expensive.

Organic Mercury Products

These materials, which are also toxic, are formulations containing only a small proportion of mercury which is in organic form and are thus much cheaper, as mercury is very expensive. The compound usually used is phenyl mercury acetate (PMA). Products available can either be mixed with water for spraying or bulked with a suitable carrier and applied dry.

Organic mercury fungicides are widely used to control fusarium patch disease and, at double rate, ophiobolus patch disease. In the latter case it is essential to wash the material right into the soil using plenty of water.

Slight scorch may be seen after using this type of fungicide, especially if insufficient water is used or if there is accidental overlapping during application. However, this is usually only a temporary yellowing of the leaf blades.

Systemic Fungicides

This type of fungicide is taken up into the plant and is to some extent distributed within it. Four compounds of this type with turf applications are benomyl, carbendazim, thiabendazole and thiophanate-methyl. These materials give good control of fusarium patch disease and are also particularly effective against dollar spot disease, especially if a nitrogenous fertilizer is also applied. They are much less toxic to man than the mercurials but are at present rather expensive.

Other Materials

Quintozene is a useful organic fungicide particularly for controlling fusarium patch disease.

Various other fungicides have applications to the turf situation, for example chlorothalonil is one of the most effective materials for the control of melting-out disease of smooth-stalked meadow-grass *(Poa pratensis)* caused by the fungus *Drechslera poae* (which used to be called *Helminthosporium vagans*).

Dichlorophen is a fungicidal compound which gives some control of fusarium patch disease, corticium disease and dollar spot disease and is also useful for moss control.

Captan and thiram are two materials used as seed dressings which give effective protection against pre-emergence damping-off.

Application

Although some of the fungicidal materials are formulated for dry application which is so very convenient, it is usually found that a more even and penetrating distribution is achieved by spraying on a suitable product. A typical volume of water would be 1120 litre/ha (100 gallons per acre). The nozzles to be used on the sprayer should be chosen with this high volume in mind and should also be sufficiently large to prevent blocking as most fungicides contain solid particles suspended in water. It is advisable to agitate the mixture to prevent settling of the solids. A better mix is usually obtained if a paste is made with a small amount of water before the bulk of the water is added.

Calibration of the spraying equipment using the nozzles chosen should be carried out by the operator who is to make the fungicidal application.

Fungicide Tolerance

Repeated use of a particular fungicidal material may lead to the development of strains of fungus which are less affected by the compound. Therefore it is a good idea to change the material used from time to time.

Safety Considerations

As with other chemicals used in turf management, an essential preliminary to all fungicidal applications is 'Read the Label', not only to ascertain the correct rate of material to use but equally importantly to discover the safety precautions to be observed. The manufacturer's instructions should be scrupulously followed at all times. Common sense precautions in handling these materials are essential even with materials thought to be of low toxicity. A particularly dangerous time is the handling of the powder or concentrate before mixing with water or when the dry formulations are mixed with their carrier and rubber gloves should be worn.

III. CORTICIUM OR RED THREAD DISEASE

Symptoms

This disease is very common on many different types of sports turf in this country. It is one of the easiest diseases to recognise once it is well established. The causal fungus is *Corticium fuciforme*. The symptoms of attack by this fungus which are most conspicuous are the production, on the infected area of grass, of 'red threads'. These are branched or unbranched needles of antler-like structure, varying from pale pink to dark red in colour. When dry they are brittle but if wet can become gelatinous. These 'needles' can spread the disease, and also allow the fungus to survive unfavourable conditions as they are quite long lived and resistant to drying out. If these 'needles' are present identification of the disease is very easy but if they are not, e.g. in the early stages of an attack, it can be more difficult. Typically the patch of affected turf has an irregular outline, in contrast to the usually well defined edges of spots caused by dollar spot disease. In addition the leaves of the grass often are most affected near the tips rather than deep in the turf. On close examination it may be possible even in the absence of needles to see some pinkish colour as the fungus mycelium can produce pink pigment.

Grasses and areas affected

Although many species of grass can be attacked by this disease, most frequently the affected species is red fescue, *Festuca rubra*. In addition, however, serious attacks may occur on perennial ryegrass, *Lolium perenne*, and it may occur on 'Highland' bent. The turf areas most frequently affected tend to be those with low fertility, especially if they are low in available nitrogen, e.g. golf fairways and cricket outfields which normally do not receive much fertilizer. Often the disease is not too serious and the grasses recover with improved growing conditions but occasionally the attack may result in death of the grass.

Prevention

As the disease is favoured by low fertility much can be done to lessen the risk of attack by maintaining the fertility of the turf, especially with regard to nitrogen. However, care is needed with fertilization. If heavy doses of nitrogen are given in autumn (when the disease is often active) whilst alleviating the problem of red thread they may lead to infection of the grass by *Fusarium nivale*. This means replacing one disease by another more serious one! In addition, over-application of fertiliser to fine turf containing a high proportion of fescue, which is the type of turf often attacked, can lead to soil conditions favouring invasion by undesirable annual meadow-grass.

Corticium can be found at any time of year but is most frequent in summer and autumn. Attack by this disease is not restricted to particular weather conditions and the best safeguard against the disease is a vigorous healthy turf.

Cure

If an attack does occur, often little is done about it, especially if the damage to the grass is not severe. In such cases careful watch should be kept on the progress of the disease and if it appears that the damage done is increasing then control measures should be applied. The two methods of dealing with this disease are:

(*a*) application of fertilizer, mainly nitrogenous, or
(*b*) application of fungicide.

In some cases a combination of the two is used. Usually the application of fertilizer at the right time results in considerable improvement in the turf but the points referred to above concerning fertilization should be kept in mind. On areas of turf of higher fertility, or if the disease appears to be doing a great deal of damage, fungicide application should be made. The inorganic mercury fungicides, i.e. mixtures of mercuric chloride (corrosive sublimate) and mercurous chloride (calomel), of which there are several commercially available brands, are very effective in controlling red thread. However, such fungicides are expensive. The organic mercury compounds (e.g. phenyl mercury acetate) have given variable results in trials on this disease, sometimes being successful, but they can not be relied upon to give effective control.

The term damping-off disease is applied to a variety of fungal diseases of seedling grass. These are divided into two groups, pre-emergence and post-emergence, depending on whether infection takes place before or after the seedlings have emerged from the soil. Large numbers of fungi can be isolated from diseased seedlings and some of these can be carried on seed. Because of the variety of fungi which can be troublesome, generalisations about the disease need to be interpreted with care since they may not apply to a particular disease outbreak.

Pre-Emergence Damping-Off

In this case infection of the seed or seedling occurs and because of this emergence is prevented. Among many fungi isolated from diseased plants are species of *Fusarium* and *Drechslera*. In normal conditions it is likely that some plants are lost to such fungal attack. The disease only becomes a problem when large numbers of plants are affected. The number and types of fungi in different soils varies and the amount of damage will also depend on environmental factors such as soil moisture and temperature. The difficulty in practice for the greenkeeper or groundsman is knowing whether this disease is present or not since poor 'take' of seedlings may be due to a variety of factors apart from fungal disease, e.g. low germination of the seed or poor growing conditions.

The damage caused by pre-emergence damping-off can be minimised by providing good growing conditions in order that the seedlings do not remain underground exposed to the pathogenic fungi for a long period. The sooner that emergence occurs the better, thus it is necessary to have correct temperature and moisture levels in the seed bed and to avoid sowing the seed either too early or too late in the year.

Fungicidal seed dressings can increase the number of seedlings that emerge. Their effect is usually most marked when small-seeded turfgrasses are sown especially in early spring when soil temperatures are low. Much, however, depends on the fungal population in the soil and this is an unknown factor in practice. However, captan and thiram at around 0.5% of seed weight have

45

proved beneficial in small scale trials. Seed ready-dressed with suitable fungicides is available commercially.

Post-Emergence Disease

As in the case of pre-emergence diseases, many fungi can be isolated from seedling turf with post-emergence diseases. They include various species of *Fusarium, Pythium* and *Cladochytrium.* The typical symptoms of post-emergence damage are small patches of yellow, bronze or red in the turf where seedlings are dying. These patches can spread rapidly and large areas can become affected.

No type of turfgrass is resistant to all post-emergence diseases but the small-seeded grasses are usually more likely to be attacked than the larger seeded ones. In the case of smooth-stalked meadow-grass *(Poa pratensis)* it is quite common for the seedlings to be attacked by *Drechslera poae,* the organism which is responsible for melting out in established smooth-stalked meadow-grass turf. If smooth-stalked meadow-grass sowings are made a careful watch should be kept for this fungus and it is necessary to choose cultivars with as much resistance as possible.

Prevention

Trouble is most likely to occur if the seed bed has not been prepared properly. Attention to drainage is of the utmost importance especially if the soil is at all heavy.

Correct fertilization will help the grass to grow through the susceptible period more rapidly and thus minimise damage.

Another important factor is seed rate and evenness of sowing. If seed is sown at too high a rate damage is more likely as the seedlings are weakened due to competition between themselves for light and nutrients. In addition, if disease does occur spread of the fungus is facilitated by the nearness of one plant to another. Dense stands of seedlings tend to create a moist surface layer of still air which is conducive to development of *Fusarium* spp.

If the surface is very wet, *Pythium* spp. and *Cladochytrium caespitis* are favoured but if the conditions are merely moist then *Fusarium* spp. are more likely to be damaging. Moist conditions favouring *Fusarium* may be produced by allowing the grass to grow too long and it is essential not to leave the young grass uncut for long periods. The first cut should be made as soon as practicable.

Control

Damping-off of seedlings can be checked by Cheshunt compound at 34 g in 3 litre/m² (1 oz in ½ gallon water per sq yd). This however, means large quantities of water and if conditions are already too wet this may not be advisable. In addition it is rather difficult in practice to use this treatment if large areas are involved. The difficulty in controlling post-emergence damping-off is that since a wide range of fungi may be involved a very wide spectrum fungicide is required if control is to be guaranteed.

One suitable material is an inorganic mercury fungicide, i.e. a mixture of mercurous and mercuric chlorides. This usually controls damping-off but must be used with care since if too high a rate is used damage can be expected as seedlings are rather less tolerant of mercury than are established plants. If conditions are wet it is often better to use dry formulations even though these may be more difficult to apply evenly.

Other fungicides, for example organic mercury products, can be used and for some damping-off diseases these will achieve satisfactory control; however, they may not work in all cases. It is often difficult to decide which fungus is responsible and it is not unusual for several fungi to be causing damage simultaneously. However, since the disease can spread very rapidly if conditions are suitable, it may be advisable to apply some fungicide at once rather than to wait for laboratory tests to identify the organism(s).

V. DOLLAR SPOT DISEASE

Dollar spot disease is caused by the fungus *Sclerotinia homoeocarpa*. In much of Europe and in the U.S.A. a wide range of turfgrass species are commonly affected. Fortunately, however, in the United Kingdom the disease is restricted to a few cultivars or natural varieties of red fescue *(Festuca rubra)*. This results in the disease being uncommon and almost entirely restricted to areas sown with susceptible cultivars of fescue or, more usually, planted with turf cut originally from the coastal salt marshes.

Symptoms

The early stages of the disease can be difficult to distinguish from the early stages of red thread (caused by *Corticium fuciforme*). As the disease progresses, however, the damage done by dollar spot is more marked, often resulting in the death of affected plants. Kill down to the soil surface is usual and this produces the characteristic overall symptoms of the disease – a number of small spots the size of a dollar or up to about 50 mm (2 in) in diameter. If many such spots are produced they can join at their edges to form extensive patches but this is less common. On some occasions a less typical infection may occur where scattered plants throughout the turf are infected without producing the distinctive 'spotty' appearance.

A further difficulty in diagnosis of this disease is that it can occur at the same time as corticium (red thread) and where the red needles of this disease are seen it is often assumed that it is solely responsible for the condition of the turf. It is important to know whether or not a particular turf is likely to be susceptible and, if it is, a careful watch for dollar spot should be kept.

Factors Encouraging the Disease

(a)   Fertility

Dollar spot most commonly occurs if the grass is under stress, particularly so if the turf is low in nitrogen in spring and summer so that growth is restricted. Application of nitrogen, however, by itself is not usually sufficient to give control once the disease has become established.

(b)   Surface Moisture

Although the infection probably takes place most frequently in spring and autumn, disease activity can continue even during hot summer weather. In these circumstances the moisture necessary

48

for the fungus probably comes from dew and therefore this should be dispersed by switching as early as possible in the day.

(c) Cultivar

Among the cultivars of red fescue that are particularly susceptible to this disease in the U.K. is Golfrood. The most common kind of susceptible turf in practice is that of sea marsh origin. Active disease can be found occurring on the marshes from which the turf is being cut. Such turf can suffer from severe disease attacks when it is placed under the additional stresses of management and play. This can lead to the disappearance of the fescue and its replacement by annual meadow-grass *(Poa annua)* and various weeds.

Control

Control measures must include attention to correct maintenance procedures, particularly with regard to nitrogen levels and surface moisture. Once infection has occurred the disease is very persistent and fungicidal treatment is needed for satisfactory control in the majority of cases.

The most effective materials for the treatment of dollar spot are a group of systemic fungicides, including benomyl, carbendazim, thiabendazole, and thiophanate-methyl.

Mercurial fungicides can also be used, the inorganic types being rather more successful than the organic.

Applications may need to be repeated, especially so in the case of the mercurials. Treatment is usually most successful if made as early in the attack as possible. During the spring and summer it has been shown that better results are obtained if application of a nitrogenous fertilizer is made around the time of fungicidal treatment.

VI. FAIRY RINGS

The condition known as 'fairy ring' can be found on most types of sports turf and is caused by the presence in the soil of fungi of the type known as Basidiomycetes. A wide range of different species live in the soil and some of these affect the growth of grass.

49

Types of Fairy Ring

The types of ring seen in sports turf have been classified into three 'grades' or 'types':

Grade 1:   typically two distinct rings of dark green stimulated grass separated by a ring of bare ground, sometimes accompanied by toadstools.

Grade 2:   a single ring of stimulated dark green grass, perhaps with fruiting bodies of the fungus (e.g. mushrooms, toadstools or puff-balls).

Grade 3:   a ring of fruiting bodies, without any visible effect on the grass.

Grade 1 Fairy Rings

The Grade 1 type of ring is usually caused by a fungus called *Marasmius oreades* and is the most serious of the three types as far as the effect on the turf and playing surface is concerned. The symptoms are as described above, particularly the zone of bare ground, are usually most marked during the growing season and particularly in dry weather. The rings may sometimes be accompanied by the fruiting bodies of the fungus – in this case a type of toadstool. These usually grow to 25 to 63 mm (1 to 2½ in) in diameter, are reddish-tan in colour and occur at the inner edge of the outer green ring. The rate of increase in diameter of a ring varies but may be as much as 460 mm (1½ ft) in a year. The stimulating effect on the grass arises from the release of nutrients, particularly nitrogen. In the outer stimulated zone this release is probably due to the breakdown of the organic matter in the soil by the fungus, whilst in the inner ring it may be due to the breakdown of the fungus itself. The fungus exists as a mycelium – a mass of thread-like structures called hyphae. These are very numerous in the bare zone and alter its wetting characteristics very noticeably. Affected soil has a strong fungal smell and becomes very dry; it is also very difficult to wet, either naturally or artificially. This lack of water is probably sufficient to account for the death of the grass but there is also evidence of poisonous material being produced by the fungus.

Grade 2 Rings

Grade 2 rings are a much more common sight than Grade 1, usually being found where turf is on a soil of low fertility which means that the extra nutrients released by the fungal breakdown of the organic matter will be of more significance. However, as no damage to the grass usually occurs, these rings are not regarded as a serious problem. Grade 2 rings can be caused by a variety of species of fungi. Among those commonly seen are *Lycoperdon* spp., a type of 'puff-ball' and *Agaricus campestris,* the edible field mushroom, but many other species can be found. Whether rings show up is to some extent dependent on the weather conditions of a particular season.

Grade 3 Rings

Grade 3 rings are rings (or sometimes a scattering) of fruiting bodies of a fungus but without any noticeable effect on the grass. This condition is simply the manifestation of the activity in the soil of various fungi, many of which may be playing an important part in organic matter breakdown and the recycling of nutrients in the soil. The reason for the fruiting body is that it is a means of liberating the spores of the fungus into the air and thus spreading them to other locations. However, fruiting bodies can spoil the appearance of turf and interfere with play.

Control

Fairy rings are difficult to control. In the case of Grades 2 and 3, control measures are not usually undertaken as they often occur on large areas of low fertility turf where expense can prevent treatment. The Grade 2 rings can be hidden by application of nitrogen which will green-up the grass as a whole to a similar colour to that found in the stimulated area. Appearance of fruiting bodies in the Grade 2 and 3 rings is usually a sudden but short-lived problem. If, however, they occur on intensively managed turf, they can to some extent be suppressed by applications of organic mercury fungicides although long term control is unlikely to be achieved.

Grade 1 rings often demand special control measures. Unfortunately, no fungicidal treatment which will guarantee successful control has yet been found. The problem arises not from the resistance of the fungus but from the difficulty of getting contact between the fungicide and the mycelium, as soil heavily contaminated by mycelium is virtually unwettable. The only treatment that can be recommended with confidence is the laborious one of digging out the ring. This, of course, is feasible only if no more than one or two small rings are involved. The procedure is begun by removing the turf and, preferably, as much of the infected soil as possible from an area extending from about 300 mm (1 ft) from the outside of the outer ring to about 300 mm (1 ft) from the inside of the inner ring. The turf and soil should be placed immediately into polythene sacks and taken away to be destroyed. Care must be taken not to allow infected soil or turf to fall on unaffected grass as new rings could be started in this way. The remaining soil in the trench formed by this operation should be sterilised. This can done with a solution containing 400 ml of 40 % formaldehyde (formalin) and 35 ml of a non-ionic wetting agent in 5½ litres of water, applied to 1 m² (6 pints of 40 % formaldehyde and ½ pint wetting agent in 10 gallons of water, applied to 10 sq yd). This solution must be kept off unaffected areas because it will kill the grass. Best results demand a thorough forking of the soil before application. Immediately after the formalin has been applied the area should be covered by polythene sheeting and left for the sterilisation to occur. Implements used should be sterilised using the same solution as that used on the soil so as to prevent them from carrying infection to other areas. The cover should be left in position for about ten days (possibly longer in cold conditions) and, after its removal, the soil should be forked to allow the formaldehyde to escape. If a great deal of the mycelium was left in the soil a second treatment with formaldehyde could be made. Otherwise the soil should be left exposed to allow thorough ventilation and this may take about fourteen days or longer in cold conditions. When the formaldehyde has evaporated the trench is filled with fresh, clean soil and then turfed (or seeded).

Other methods of fairy ring control are often suggested but their evaluation is difficult as the rings can apparently disappear of their own accord. Erroneous opinions may be formed unless carefully controlled experiments are carried out.

One method suggested by Lebeau and Hawn in Canada is to attempt to wet thoroughly the affected soil. This needs spiking of the ring followed by persistent watering, for example every day for at least a month. If the soil can be made wet, the ring may gradually disappear. In the trials carried out by Lebeau and Hawn, addition of fungicide to the water used for the drenching did not seem to be any improvement over the plain water treatment.

Where large numbers of rings are found and treatment is impractical, some comfort may be taken from the suggestion made by J. Drew Smith that the incidence of rings decreases with time, the rings disappearing when they meet or come up to physical barriers.

VII.   FUSARIUM PATCH DISEASE

This disease, caused by the fungus *Fusarium nivale*, is a commonly met problem on all types of turf. It is probably the worst disease of turf, particularly fine turf, in the United Kingdom.

Recognition

Well established attacks in the growing season are not difficult to identify. The grass is killed off in large patches and in moist conditions it is often possible to see the fungus itself as pale white or pinkish threads resembling fragments of cotton wool. This is encouraged by still moist air. The necessity of recognising the disease early before much damage has been done can not be over-emphasised. The first sign is often small patches which are wet and yellow brown to dark brown in appearance. If left these will rapidly increase in size when conditions are suitable. The fungus can also be a problem under snow and the damage is then seen only after the snow has melted.

Factors Encouraging the Disease

Although attacks have been recorded in every month of the year, the most troublesome time is autumn. The climatic condition most favourable to the fungus is high humidity, as the fungus is inhibited by dry conditions. Moist turf surfaces combined with overcast weather conditions will often precipitate disease attack. Thus in such conditions it is necessary to watch carefully for the appearance of the disease. If too heavy an application of compost top dressing is made, this can also be troublesome as the grass is covered and the air around it becomes moist because the compost cover decreases evaporation of water. Such dressings should be applied carefully and worked in.

Another major factor influencing disease production is fertility. In general more akaline conditions favour the disease. One aspect of the relationship between fertility and disease is the timing of application of nitrogenous fertilizers which rapidly increase the available nitrogen content of the soil. If such fertilizers, e.g. sulphate of ammonia, are given in the autumn period, they result in a lush growth of the grass and in this state it is less resistant to fungal invasion.

Although practically all the grasses found in sports turf may be attacked by the disease, the most susceptible is annual meadow-grass *(Poa annua)* and its ubiquity is one reason the disease is so common. In turf containing a high proportion of annual meadow-grass it is essential to be on the watch for disease.

When the disease is active care should be taken not to spread it unnecessarily. The fungus produces sticky spores which are easily picked up by feet or implements and may start fresh attacks on nearby areas.

Prevention

Prevention is better than cure. The risk of disease can be reduced by paying attention to the factors influencing disease production. Removal of surplus moisture from the turf by drainage or removal of dew by switching will help, as will care in the timing of application of nitrogen. However, in some exceptional situations, e.g. where obstructions such as hedges make still moist air stand over the turf it may be impossible to prevent disease in this way. Then experience will show when disease can be expected and it is good sense to make an application of fungicide in advance to prevent the disease. However, regular preventive applications throughout the year should be avoided as there is

54

Fusarium patch disease showing clearly on dewy turf.

evidence to show that this makes for more difficulties later and also costs money!

Control

The disease can be controlled by fungical treatment. There are many suitable materials. The inorganic mercury fungicides, i.e. mixtures of mercuric and mercurous chloride, are very efficient but rather expensive and, being poisonous, must be handled with great care. The organic mercury fungicides, e.g. phenyl mercury acetate, are in common use as they are both efficient in control and cheap. They are, however, poisons and can also cause damage to grass if applied at excessive rates. They should not be used on smooth-stalked meadow-grass *(Poa pratensis)* as this grass can be scorched badly by application at the standard rate. The non-mercurial organic fungicide, quintozene, is a very useful material against this disease. In recent years systemic fungicides (based on benomyl, carbendazim, thiabendazole and thiophanate-methyl) have gained in popularity.

Fungicide application should be made as soon as the disease is observed, especially in conditions when rapid spread is likely. In suitable weather the areas affected can increase *very* rapidly (e.g. over-night) and a great deal of damage can be done. Also this damage will be difficult to repair at a time when growth is slow (e.g. in autumn).

Where the disease has been active under snow, it is only seen when the snow melts. It may then be too late to prevent damage and all that can be done is to try to get the grass growing again, to spray with fungicide so as to prevent further damage and to re-seed if necessary. If a turf area is likely to lie under snow for long periods, a preventive application of fungicide may give protection. Such treatment is best given as late as possible before the snow falls.

VIII.   SOME LEAF SPOTS OF TURFGRASSES

Careful examination of the leaves of turfgrass may reveal the presence of leaf spots. These are distinct areas of leaf which have been killed by the activities of fungi. Many different species occur and only a few of the more common ones are here discussed. In many cases little is known of the long-term effects of the damage on the botanical composition of a sward and this group of diseases, with the exception of melting-out disease of smooth-stalked meadow-grass, is often ignored in practical turfgrass situations. They may, however, be more important than is often realised.

'Melting-out' and Leaf Spot of Smooth-stalked Meadow-grass

A leaf spot and melting-out disease of smooth-stalked meadow-grass *(Poa pratensis)* can be caused by a fungus called *Drechslera poae*. This species is often still referred to, especially in the U.S.A., by its old name, *Helminthosporium vagans*. The leaf spot, which is brown or purple with a paler centre, is usually up to 9 mm long by 3 mm wide. Such leaf spots can occur on most cultivars of *P. pratensis* but in some circumstances, particularly on some cultivars, extensive damage may occur resulting in the condition known as melting-out.

56

Fungicidal treatment is possible but it is difficult to justify on an economic basis in practice because suitable fungicides (e.g. chlorothalonil) would need to be applied regularly. When new sowings are being made, the risk of disease can be lessened, but not removed entirely, by careful choice of cultivar. Where smooth-stalked meadow-grass has been growing for some time, there will already have been a natural selection for some degree of resistance as the most susceptible plants will have been killed out. The systemic fungicides in current use give no control of this disease or leaf spots caused by other *Drechslera* spp. Organic mercury fungicides cause leaf scorch on some cultivars.

It is commonly believed that close cutting makes the disease more serious and it is suggested in various American publications that the height of cut should be the maximum that use will permit. However, this practice in the U.S.A. encourages infection of the grass by other plant pathogens. Cutting height must, of course, be within the range tolerated by the grass and appropriate to the sport concerned.

Leaf Spot on Perennial Ryegrass

Perennial ryegrass *(Lolium perenne)* is affected by *Drechslera siccans (Helminthosporium siccans)*. This fungus causes an oval leaf spot, usually brown in colour, sometimes becoming pale at the centre with age. Occasionally, lesions may occur as dark streaks. Foot-rot symptoms, i.e. a similar condition to that described for melting-out, have also been reported, although there is some doubt as to whether the same fungus is always responsible, as other related species (e.g. *Drechslera dictyoides*) can also attack perennial ryegrass and identification is not always easy.

Typical attacks by *Drechslera siccans* usually show only leaf spot symptoms and the short-term damage does not seem serious. However, as a proportion of the leaf area is destroyed, growth may be reduced and the effect of this in stress situations, like wear, may be more important than is currently thought. In addition, little is known of any long-term effects of the fungus on the sward.

Altough fungicides are not usually used in practice, trials have shown that control of this disease can be achieved by using an organic mercury fungicide or chlorothalonil.

57

Leaf Spot on Fescue

Festuca rubra can be attacked by *Drechslera dictyoides*. This fungus also produces net-blotch on meadow fescue *(Festuca pratensis)* but on red fescue these symptoms are not usually seen. Instead, the lesions are usually small, red-brown in colour and irregular in shape. In some plots of single cultivars grown in trials this fungus has been found associated with dead patches of turf somewhat resembling dollar spot in overall symptoms. It is not known if *D. dictyoides* was really responsible but no other pathogens were found. It is interesting to note that in the U.S.A. this fungus does cause a serious disease of red fescue.

Timothy leaf spot

Various species of fungi can cause leaf spots on timothy *(Phleum pratense)*. One fairly common species is *Cladosporium phlei*. This produces a red-purple spot, fairly small (up to 5 mm) and often with a pale centre.

Other fungi responsible for leaf spot on timothy include *Drechslera phlei* and *Mastigosporium* spp.

Fungicidal control is not usually thought necessary.

Leaf Spot on other species of turfgrass

Most species of turfgrass can show leaf spot symptoms and a large number of fungi have been isolated from such lesions. Usually the effect does not appear to be serious on established plants, but some of these fungi are also found associated with post-emergence damping-off disease of grass seedlings where their activities may be much more serious. Most of these fungi and their effects on turfgrass need much more study and it is hoped that over the next few years knowledge of this aspect will increase. It is likely that, with such study, the number of diseases recognised on turfgrass will also increase.

IX. OPHIOBOLUS PATCH DISEASE

Ophiobolus patch disease is caused by the fungus *Gaeumannomyces graminis (Ophiobolus graminis)*. The same organism is

58

Ophiobolus patch disease showing disease resistant grass (fescue) growing in the centre of turf killed by the disease.

responsible for a disease of cereals called 'Take-all'. During the last twenty years or so, as far as turf is concerned, the disease appears either to have been increasing or at any rate to have been recognised more frequently. This disease differs from most of the other common turf diseases in that the fungus directly attacks the roots of the grass. Damage is most usually seen from mid-summer until late autumn. However the disease is perennial and will again become active on the same patches after a dormant period during winter and spring unless some curative treatment is made.

Recognition

When well established, ophiobolus patch disease can be recognised without too much difficulty. Typically the most obvious symptom is a ring of grass which is being killed and appears a bronzed or yellow colour. The species most frequently attacked is

59

browntop bent *(Agrostis tenuis)* although other turfgrasses may be affected. The susceptibility of bent aids in the recognition of the disease because within the area surrounded by the ring of current fungus activity very little of this grass is to be found, its place being occupied instead by other grasses, for example fescue, annual meadow-grass or rough-stalked meadow-grass and by broad-leaved weeds, commonly including pearlwort *(Sagina procumbens)* and mouse-ear chickweed *(Cerastium vulgatum)*. This weed-filled centre to the rings often makes them recognisable even when the fungus is dormant and the yellow ring is not visible.

Factors Encouraging Disease Incidence

In the past, disease activity was thought to be encouraged by wet conditions and seemed to be most common in the moister north-western parts of the country. In addition the disease has usually been associated with liming of over-acid turf, for example golf fairways at pH 4.0-4.5 containing a high proportion of bent. However, increasingly, cases are being reported which do not fit these management and climatic patterns. Indeed, the disease is now sometimes seen on sandy golf greens which have free-draining properties and which have been maintained at a pH appropriate for fine turf (pH 5.0-6.0). The spread, however, may be in part at least due to the increasing use of artificial watering systems on these free-draining soils which give a higher water availability during the summer. However, it is also known that *G. graminis* is affected by other soil fungi; factors which alter the balance between them and *G. graminis* may lead to an increase in disease activity. One extreme example of this arises from sterilisation of soil with methyl bromide, a process which is occasionally carried out during the pre-seeding preparation of golf greens in order that a weed-free seed bed can be obtained. On such greens ophiobolus patch disease has sometimes followed soon after establishment. This is believed to be due to the absence of a balanced state between various soil fungi as the sterilisation procedure has killed all the fungi originally present in the soil.

Control Measures

Since experience has shown that liming of turf can lead to serious outbreaks of the disease, applications of lime should only be made where analysis of the soil shows that it is absolutely necessary. In addition, management of the turf should be such that extreme over-acidity is avoided thus also removing the need for liming.

Where fungicidal treatment of the disease is considered necessary it is very important to remember that infection is occurring on the roots of the grass so that penetration of the fungicide into the root zone is essential. In Britain the fungicides most usually used for ophiobolus patch disease control are those containing organic mercury compounds. The rate used is twice that recommended for fusarium patch disease and it is important to use sufficient water, following the maker's instructions. Reducing the volume of water will reduce the likelihood of successful control and may lead to leaf scorch, especially in hot conditions. It is often beneficial to disturb the surface of the turf, e.g. by spiking, to encourage penetration of the fungicide into the soil. Normally at least two, and possibly three, applications will be needed, separated by intervals of 10–14 days.

The systemic fungicides which have been introduced during the last few years have in trials shown mixed results and until more information can be obtained anyone wishing to use these materials for ophiobolus patch disease should try them out on small areas to begin with.

In the United States of America claims have been made that control can be achieved by using chlordane but British experience has been that, both in disease control trials and on areas receiving chlordane for worm control, good results against ophiobolus patch disease were not obtained.

A possible alternative to fungicidal treatment on areas where the expense is too great to face, e.g. where whole fairways are affected, is to apply fertilizer of a type which has an acidifying effect so as to make the immediate environment of the root more acid and thus less favourable to the fungus and also to encourage growth of the turfgrass. Such application should of course only be made at an appropriate time of year.

DRAG BRUSH

Ordinary brushes or brooms will not perform satisfactorily the work of a drag brush. This has a specially shaped head with long stiff bristles which used to be of whalebone but are now of plastic which is less brittle. A drag brush is pulled along to work top dressings into flat turf surfaces such as cricket tables, tennis courts and flat bowling greens. It is also useful for dispersal of dew and worm casts and for gentle scarification to bring prostrate growth up for mowing off (usually at right angles to the brushing) or to help control the 'nap' which may occur on some fine turf. Brushes of suitable sizes – 1.2—2.4 m (4—8 ft.) – may be pulled by hand or by some convenient power unit.

DRAG MAT

Rather resembling some kinds of shoe scraper, a drag mat is a flexible steel mat which is pulled along to work in top dressings, more particularly on turf surfaces where undulations are appropriate, e.g. golf greens, crown bowling greens. It may also be used for dispersing dew or worm casts. It is self-cleaning on reversal. Sizes – usually 910—1220 mm (3—4 ft.) – are available for hand pulling or for machine pulling.

DRAINAGE

I. GENERAL

To provide good playing facilities, especially for winter games, well drained turf is essential. Experience has shown that winter pitches with consistently dry turf will withstand a large amount of play and only need minor renovations (e.g. to goal areas and centre circle of soccer pitches) at the end of the season whilst a

62

Drag Mat.

wet pitch soon becomes a mud bath after little play and therefore often requires major renovations at the season's end. The problem of providing good, hard wearing pitches can usually be resolved into one of ensuring adequate drainage. Whilst the effects of bad drainage are most conspicuous on winter pitches, good drainage is also very important for golf courses as well as for bowling greens and other areas used mainly in the summer. Drainage is not simply a matter of installing pipes and it is important to have some appreciation of various other factors which have relevance to drainage problems on existing turf areas.

The most important practical aspects of ensuring freedom from surplus water are:

1. the prevention of water from higher ground flowing to the site over the surface or below ground;
2. getting the water away from the immediate sub-soil;
3. getting rainwater away from the surface, i.e. through the top soil (and, as appropriate, the sub-soil also) quickly.

The first may require the construction along the boundaries of ditches or catchwater drains of sufficient depth to intercept any flow of water entering the site over the surface or along water bearing strata.

The second is a question of under drainage as commonly understood. The problem on sportsfields is usually more one of effectively removing surface water percolating through or remaining on the top soil than one of controlling a rising water table. Occasionally, though rarely, sites are encountered where there is a naturally free draining sub-soil of sand or gravel, but on most sites the installation of a land drainage system is essential.

The third aspect is the one which is most often not fully understood or appreciated. It involves the permeability of the top soil which is conditioned by soil texture and soil structure and which is affected by treatment during construction as well as during maintenance and use. It also involves the sub-soil which is probably little affected by use but may have been severely compacted during construction.

The over-all rate of drainage is that of the slowest drainage layers and it is important that during construction there should be adequate sub-soil cultivation as well as top soil cultivation. Sub-soil cultivation has been known to be successful on established playing fields with a built in sub-soil compaction problem but it can be so disruptive as to destroy the turf completely – the work must be done during construction.

Soil Texture

The ideal playing field has a sandy, open-textured soil with good natural drainage. In practice, of course, whatever land is available has usually to be used for sports turf purposes, irrespective of suitability. When constructing playing fields on relatively heavy land, large quantities of sand are sometimes worked into the surface soil to improve the texture and such treatment, although expensive, can be very successful in helping drainage.

Soil Structure

A soil with a good structure which contains many small spaces between soil crumbs drains well because the water has plenty of room to move through the comparatively large pores. Soil structure is easily lost if the soil aggregates are squeezed together and broken down – as can happen if the land is worked or used in any way when too wet. When this happens the permeability of the soil may fall to less than a tenth of its 'natural' level. During construction of new sports areas this factor is all too often overlooked in the rush to achieve completion and were it not for the fact that grass roots do such a good job of soil structure improvement there would be more trouble than we have already. Use of winter pitches is such that play damages the structure of the top soil and, of course, deterioration is progressive. The condition is extremely difficult to remedy – without complete reconstruction and soil improvement.

Soil Structure Improvement

From time to time various chemical soil additives for improving the structure of soils have been suggested. However, there seems little evidence that when used on playing fields any of them have shown any great improvements in soil structure or drainage. To date the best way of maintaining or improving soil structure and thus drainage is to grow a strongly rooted turf since this is one of the finest soil structure-forming agents known. The situation is, of course, further helped by attention to all other aspects of turf maintenance. Spiking and forking are of immense direct benefit in getting surplus water away from the surface quickly with consequent improvement in playing conditions and reduced surface damage but their effect on soil structure is slow and indirect.

Solving Drainage Problems

Different types of drainage are described under their appropriate headings and they are all expensive. Whether constructing new sports turf areas or trying to improve old ones it is essential to get expert advice on drainage with a view to getting value for money as well as to achieving success.

New areas almost invariably need a pipe drainage system – if money is available there may be a case for a drainage layer also. To ensure that under heavy use surplus water gets from the surface to the drains consideration should be given to the main alternatives:– massive amelioration of the top soil with sand or installation of slit drainage – or any possible combination.

If massive amelioration is decided upon the right amount of the right kind of sand has to be incorporated into the top soil during cultivations. Whether or no soil amelioration is decided upon it is wise to design a drainage system that will accommodate future slit drainage if this proves necessary. There are decided practical difficulties in introducing slit drainage during construction and so it is usually postponed until the turf is established (and possibly the need proved!).

When considering improvement of existing wet sports areas careful investigation of all the circumstances is necessary and the first requirement is that there should be an efficient pipe drainage scheme. If there are no drains already there, a system will have to be put in (or on rare occasions mole drainage installed).

If there is an existing drainage system and there are no severe compaction problems left over from the construction period it is surprising what degree of benefit can be obtained from enthusiastic use of appropriate aeration equipment. If there is a sub-soil 'pan' then sub-soil cultivation can be considered to alleviate the condition. This has proved successful on many occasions but involves considerable risk of wrecking the turf completely and so involving re-seeding.

66

Whilst mixing sand through the whole top soil of existing turf is impracticable, top dressing with sand can be helpful in opening up the immediate surface and providing improved traction. Sand may also, to some degree, be worked into hollow tine fork holes to help maintain free passage of water from the surface.

If bad drainage persists then an appropriate type of slit drainage provides a very good answer. The process is, unfortunately, not cheap and the main problem may be finding the money to do it.

II. PIPE DRAINAGE

Planning a Pipe Drainage System

Systems of pipe drainage are herringbone, grid, fan-shaped, catchwater (cut-off) and 'natural' (following existing contours). Some form of herringbone system is usually appropriate for sports ground use but a modified grid system is often suitable for single football pitches, tennis courts or bowling greens whilst a catchwater (cut-off) system may be needed on any ground, possibly in addition to the main system.

When planning sports turf drainage systems various factors have to be taken into account and the position of suitable outfalls is the first thing to look for. The direction and steepness of the falls of the land govern the type of layout chosen while the intensity of the drainage will be governed by the soil type and by economics. When, as is often the case, the hydraulic conductivities of all the soil layers under field conditions are unknown, then experience is used in deciding the depth and spacing of the drains.

Common playing field practice, based on experience, is to lay main drains 760 mm (2 ft 6 in) deep with the steepest fall, with laterals at about 610 mm (2 ft) depth and at an angle of 45° or 60° to the mains. This enables the laterals to intercept water flowing down the main slope and also gives some fall along laterals, which can be placed at a constant depth thus reducing the amount of work involved in producing the drain trenches. On near level sites some grading of the trenches may be necessary since laterals should not be laid with a fall of less than 1 in 300 and

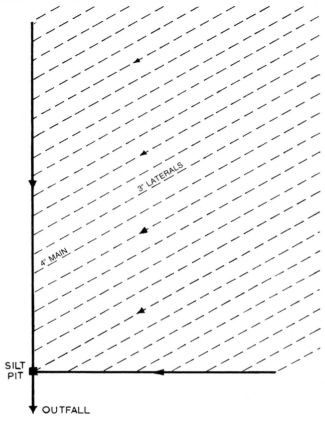

Grid system of drainage.

it is better to aim at a minimum of 1 in 200, preferably uniform. The laterals are joined to the main drain by purpose-made junctions.

On light soils laterals may be as much as 7.5–12.0 m (25–40 ft) apart whereas on heavy soil, where available funds allow, 3.0–4.5 m (9–15 ft) apart is more appropriate. The drains are backfilled to within 150–225 mm (6–9 in) of the surface with a coarse aggregate (graded clinker, gravel, etc.) blinded with gritty ash, coarse sand or fine gravel. Over the backfill top soil only is placed.

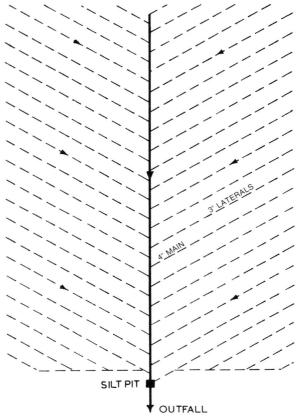

SILT PIT ■

▼ OUTFALL

Herringbone system of drainage.

Summary of important points to bear in mind when organising a drainage system.

(a) The need for a good outlet.

(b) The possible need for perimeter catchwater drains to cut off water from surrounding land.

(c) The line of the main drains should usually be in the direction of the main fall of the land.

(d) If the field has been graded to even falls, the mains can be laid at a constant depth – usually 760 mm (2 ft 6 in), i.e. if the slope of the field is 1 : 60 the fall on the main drain is 1 : 60. With the laterals also laid to a constant depth

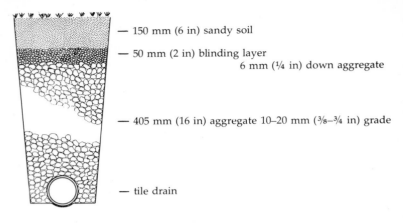

— 150 mm (6 in) sandy soil

— 50 mm (2 in) blinding layer
                    6 mm (¼ in) down aggregate

— 405 mm (16 in) aggregate 10–20 mm (⅜–¾ in) grade

— tile drain

Section of tile drain.

(610 mm [2 ft]) the fall along their lines will be less as they are laid across the line of the maximum fall at an angle to the main (approximately 1 : 85 if the laterals are at an angle of 45°). On a level site it will be necessary to construct a fall along the drain runs – say 1 : 200.

(e) Drain trenches should be excavated cleanly to the appropriate width in straight lines.

(f) Sub-soil excavated from the drain runs should be removed immediately and not allowed to remain at the side of the trench to contaminate the top soil.

(g) Pipes may be clayware or perforated plastic. Clayware laterals are usually 75 mm (3 in), sub-mains 100 mm (4 in) and mains from 100 mm (4 in) upwards according to circumstances. Plastic pipes are usually supplied to somewhat smaller dimensions based on claims that they will carry water more efficiently than clayware pipes (i.e. ordinary land tiles).

(h) Clayware pipes should be laid with closely butted joints and the end pipes of each drain run should be sealed. Plastic pipes should be properly joined and stop ends inserted at the head ends of runs.

(i) Purpose made junctions of the appropriate sizes should be used for connecting laterals to mains.

(j)   The selection of the backfill material is very important; the material chosen should allow water to pass through it quickly and moreover retain this quality for many years. Single sized 12.5 mm (½ in) or 18 mm (¾ in) gravel is very suitable and this should be blinded with 50 mm (2 in) suitable coarse sand. (Suitable grades of clinker may be used instead of gravel and sand.)

The final level of the backfill is normally brought up to within 150 mm (6 in) of the surface and then covered with top soil.

(k)   Keep duplicate plans showing the drainage system organised, the drains actually installed and any subsequent alterations.

III. MOLE DRAINAGE

The introduction of a tile drainage system into an ill drained playing area is very costly and, in some circumstances, mole drainage can provide an acceptable and cheaper alternative. Mole drainage can also be used to supplement existing tile drainage. It is rarely, if ever, used when constructing new sports turf areas.

What is it?

Mole drainage involves a system of mechanically produced tubular channels in the sub-soil. It is installed by drawing a 50–100 mm (2–4 in) diameter bullet shaped steel 'mole' with trailing expander through the sub-soil at a predetermined depth. The mole is fitted to the lower end of a vertical blade and as a result of the operation a drainage channel is formed which is linked to the surface by a slit.

Soil type required for success

The channels created by pulling the mole plough through the sub-soil will only persist and be of use if the soil within that region of the profile has a clay consistency. Effective mole channels are unlikely to be formed in a stony, peaty, sandy or shale soil; hence care must be taken to check that there are no hidden local outcrops of such materials on the land to be drained.

Formation of Channel

For a rigid, smooth-walled mole channel to be formed, the work is best carried out whilst the sub-soil is in a moist, plastic condition. It is preferable, however, that the top soil is fairly dry so that surface damage is minimised on existing grassland. Sometimes it is worth while feeding pea gravel into the slits to keep open a permanent passage for surface water to get away.

As with tile drains, the mole channels must have a good fall along their length (minimum 1 : 200) and this is usually achieved by using the fall of the land. It can be seen, therefore, that a flat site will be very difficult to mole drain. Drawing the moles uphill has certain advantages if convenience and layout of the site allows.

Depth and Distance

To increase the chances of longer life, the mole channels should be formed some distance (say 150 mm [6 in]) below the usual transition zone of clay sub-soil and the more friable top soil. Drawing the channels at 450–500 mm (18–20 in) depth is generally suitable, thus avoiding, it is hoped, any unsuspected tile drains, but with channels deep enough to escape damage from heavy traffic. In agriculture the maximum length of a mole 'run' is about 200 m (220 yd), if suitable falls allow.

For mole drainage to be really effective the channels must be close together, suitable intervals being 2–5 m (6–15 ft) according to the severity of the drainage problem. Where wet 'ridge and furrow' land exists, the mole channel is best introduced into the furrow.

Outlets

Each mole channel should be provided with an outlet. This can be done by one of the following methods:

(a) Drawing the mole channels into a ditch. It is important however, that there should be continuous clearance of drainage water from within the ditch. It is also advisable to insert a few lengths of pipe into the last couple of metres of the mole channel approaching the entry into the ditch. This prevents collapse of the vulnerable end section of the mole drain.

(b) Drawing each mole channel through the porous aggregate overlying a tile drain. The mole channels should be about 50–75 mm (2–3 in) above the tile drain which could be specially introduced for the purpose, or could form part of an existing tile drainage system.

Pros and cons

A mole drainage system introduced into a wet playing area can bring about great improvement. The slit formed by the vertical blade of the mole plough which may persist to some degree for a very long time allows surface water to pass freely to the drain below. A properly formed mole drainage system in heavy clay soil should remain quite efficient for 6–7 years, and it is not unknown for useful service to be obtained for double this length of time. It can not, however, be regarded as permanent.

Besides not being a permanent solution to a drainage problem, there are other disadvantages to mole draining. During installation surface damage of existing turf can be considerable, particularly when the work is performed by an inexperienced operator and/or under the wrong soil conditions. Humps resulting from the heave of the mole plough passing through the soil usually produce an undulating surface for some time and in drought conditions the new slits can widen appreciably.

Generally speaking the main advantage of mole drainage is cheapness and it is comparatively rarely used for sports turf except occasionally on golf fairways which do not have heavy traffic over them.

IV. SLIT DRAINAGE

Intensive use of sports turf (particularly under wet conditions) and some maintenance practices cause compaction of the surface soil and breakdown of crumb structure. This ultimately results in the soil transmitting water very slowly and so there is increased

73

wetness – and more damage. A new solution to this problem involves 'by-passing' the soil by means of slit drainage.

Slit drainage, a process introduced into Britain by the Sports Turf Research Institute, provides a means for surplus water to get away from the surface without working its way through the body of the top soil. This is achieved by producing slits in the earth which are then filled to the surface with permeable material down which water can pass freely to find its way into more permeable conditions and to the drains (except in the rare case where sub-surface conditions are such that drains are not required at all).

A good drainage system is usually an essential pre-requisite to efficient slit drainage.

The possibilities for the use of slit drainage on fine turf areas seem very limited because of the very high (and uniform) standards of surface required but many excellent results have been obtained on winter pitches. Slit drainage has also been used successfully on golf fairways and approaches.

There are practical difficulties in introducing slit drainage during construction of new pitches mainly because of the difficulty of getting a good seed bed without burying the tops of the slits and thus nullifying most of their value. One way out of the dilemma which has been used on a very few pitches so far is to use wide slits (as described below) and to produce a seed bed in a specially produced and *extremely* sandy layer about 50 mm (2 in) deep. This means that above the slits there is a deliberately placed protective layer of very permeable material which is emptied by the slits and the layer can be 'refreshed' as necessary with extra sand. Slit drainage is, however, most commonly used on inadequately drained existing pitches.

Types of Slit Drainage

There are two main types of slit drainage:

1. In the cheaper type quite narrow (about 12 mm [½ in]) slits are used. They are produced by a special type of machine known as a sand injector which forms the slit with a vibrating steel coulter and feeds sand into the space. There are two sizes of machine, a large tractor-drawn one and a smaller self-propelled machine.

74

Slit draining. 50 mm (2 in) wide slits are being produced mechanically.

These 'sand injection' slits may be about 175 mm (7 in) deep or more but there is no earth excavated. Optimum spacing may vary but very good results have been achieved with 300 mm (12 in) spacings – wider spacings may sometimes suffice.

The surface of the turf sometimes becomes ridged but settles down remarkably well over a period of a few months. This kind of slit drainage has been used successfully on many winter pitches (including League soccer grounds).

The narrow slits carry water vertically downwards very satis-factorily but they have very little capacity for lateral transmission so as to take the water to the drains. For best results from narrow slit drainage it is therefore necessary for the slits to reach an extremely permeable sub-soil (which is rare) or a drainage layer of gravel or clinker emptied by drains. If neither of these is available it may be possible to organise a system in which narrow

75

slits are used in conjunction with a limited number of wide slits such as described below and at least a skeleton system of drains.

2.   Wider slits, usually about 50 mm (2 in) wide, are produced by suitable narrow trenching machines which excavate out the earth which then has to be removed from site. The trench is filled to the surface with suitable permeable material. Depth, spacing and type of filling in the trenches are inter-related. The usual depth is about 150-225 mm (6-9 in), so as to link with the drains, although the machines can go deeper if required. As with narrow slits optimum spacing is not firmly resolved but 600 mm (2 ft) is being widely adopted.

Fifty mm (2 in) slits filled to the surface with permeable material offer ready passage for surplus water to get away from the surface. With suitable types of filling they can afford sufficient lateral transmission of water to the fill over the drains. If the wide slits link with a drainage layer they can be filled entirely with sand. Usually, however, they are required to link to the fill over drains and then the bottom of the trench needs to be filled with suitable gravel (e.g. pea gravel) covered with suitable matching sand. With knowledge of the amount of water the system is designed to cope with and the distance apart of the drains it is possible to calculate the depth of gravel needed, the remainder of the trench being filled with sand. There are, however, problems if the drains are too far apart or lack sufficient good backfill and when a new drainage system is installed it is advisable to bear in mind possible future slit drainage.

Some Problems Associated with Slit Drainage

So long as the sand-topped slits are open to the surface they take away surface water quickly. They also attract water from the body of the soil but they can not dry beyond field capacity and, at this, some soils might still not be too satisfactory until dried further by evaporation. This does not seem to have affected a very good success record so far!

Since the slits are filled up with sand (possibly with gravel below) the colour and vigour of grass growing on or near the slits could be affected but this has to date not been very conspicuous.

League football clubs have so far regarded with suspicion wide slits brought right to the surface because of possible effects on play and players of the variation in surface consistency which they confer.

The length of time that slits will continue to give really marked drainage benefits is uncertain and would certainly seem to be limited. Below ground there seems little reason why the slits should not exist indefinitely unless mechanically dispersed. The problem lies in keeping free contact with the surface since they are liable to get covered over with up to 25 mm (1 in) of the original impermeable material. If this happens the slits have not lost all their value but they have lost a great deal of it. Methods of coping with the problem include over-filling with sand in the first place, top dressing with sand – and repeated slitting! In the latter connection it has been reported that there is now a machine which will efficiently produce shallow (and narrow) sand slits to restore the connection between the main slits and the surface.

V. AIR DRAINAGE

The maintenance of a free flow of air across a turf surface helps considerably in drying it out to the advantage of the playing surface. Moreover, reducing the humidity around the foliage discourages disease. Air movement should be promoted by leaving suitable gaps in hedges, fences and buildings surrounding a turf area. The term 'air drainage' is a convenient way of indicating requirements.

DROUGHT RESISTANCE

The resistance of turf to drought depends on a combination of factors which include: kind and depth of soil, soil acidity and fertility, kind of grass and the way it is being grown.

For best drought resistance a deep fertile soil which is not excessively acid is important. Sandy soils, so popular for good drainage, are not usually good for drought resistance.

Some grasses, e.g. fine fescues, are more drought resistant than others. Height of cut is also important – cutting short imposes stress on the grass which becomes the more sensitive to other stresses such as shortage of water. If it is not possible to apply sufficient water during dry weather it is a good plan to cut the grass less closely than normal and to allow the cuttings to fly so that they can act as a moisture retaining mulch. A helpful mulch may also be provided by top dressing. Good root development is important since the more root there is the greater the amount of soil explored for water.

Turf with excess of fibre (mat or thatch) at the surface lacks drought resistance, partly because rain water penetration into the soil and to the roots is restricted by the fibre which holds it, possibly until it is evaporated away.

All turf grasses seem to have a remarkable resistance to drought as was seen after the record 1976 drought.

EARLY CARE OF NEW TURF AREAS

(see also ESTABLISHMENT)

At the time that establishment has been completed on new sports turf areas it is important that staff, equipment and materials are available for the specially important maintenance during the first year or so – the development period. During this time there may well be no use of the new facility and all too frequently this results in omission to organise satisfactory arrangements.

A.   *Sown Land*

The first cut (and sometimes the second also) is often included in the contract (when there is one).

Fine Turf

When the grass has reached about 50 mm (2 in) in height any stones left on the surface are picked off and usually a light rolling carried out to firm up the earth around the seedlings and to press any remaining small stones into the ground. When the grass has regained the vertical it should be carefully topped with a sharp mower preferably of the side wheel or possibly the rotary type. Only about 12.5 mm (½ in) should be removed at this stage but with succeeding cuts the height of cut is gradually lowered to about 12.5 mm (½ in) and maintained there by regular mowing (three times per week) for some months until the turf has become well established. It can then be lowered gradually to the final height wanted.

With the preferred late summer sowing only one or two cuts are normally required before winter weather checks growth and no fertilizer or other treatment is normally required until the spring.

As the weather improves in the spring and there is appreciable growth mowing should commence and, in due course, a complete fertilizer applied (see FERTILIZERS). During the summer further fertilizer of a nitrogenous kind should be given at intervals of about four weeks if necessary, the aim being to achieve a strong turf of the sown grasses as quickly as possible. Spring sown turf also needs the follow up fertilizer treatments.

Top dressing should be carried out at least two or three times with a view to producing a smooth surface which allows close cutting and which is necessary for the game to be played.

A close watch for disease should be kept up right from the beginning so that treatment can be applied immediately it is required. Worm and weed control may also be needed.

General Turf Areas (Winter Pitches etc.)

The main needs are again mowing and feeding. The first cut should be carried out after stone picking and rolling when the grass has grown to about 75 mm (3 in), only about 25 mm (1 in) being removed at this stage. The height of cut is then gradually lowered to about 25 mm (1 in) and maintained there for the whole of the summer by *regular* mowing. As with fine turf it is important to keep grass growing so as to get strong establishment of sown grasses as quickly as possible and to this end dressings of fertilizer should be applied from time to time as required. Weed control may also be needed.

B. *Turfed Areas*

Turfing is usually undertaken only on fine turf areas such as bowling greens and cricket tables. Top dressing is the operation which completes the actual turf laying phase and further top dressing is required at intervals throughout the whole of the first year in order to achieve the perfectly smooth surface required for the game and which permits close cutting. Regular mowing (three times a week during the main growing season) is important, the height to which the grass can be taken down being regulated by the smoothness of the surface but really close mowing is usually not advisable until well on in the summer. At this time some preliminary light rolling may be started on cricket tables. There is usually need for one or two dressings of fertilizer during the first year but over-feeding should be avoided. If good turf has been purchased there should be no need for weedkilling but there could be need for worming at the end of the summer. A close watch for signs of disease should be maintained at all times.

ESTABLISHMENT

(see also CONSTRUCTION and EARLY CARE)

A. *Establishment from Seed*

Establishment of turf is normally intended to be on a permanent basis and, once the grass is there, severe limitations are imposed on what can be achieved in the way of soil improvement or cultivation. It is therefore obviously important to get the top soil into good condition before sowing grass seed.

Cultivations

Thorough cultivations are essential. For small areas this means digging followed by work with hand cultivators and hand rakes, stone picking, heeling etc. For large areas thorough application of the 'old fashioned' approach involving the use of ploughs, tine cultivators and disc, spike and chain harrows is usually the best. It is advantageous if cultivations can take place over a period of some weeks in the summer so as to give a period of fallowing with a view to eliminating as many weeds as possible. In the final stages of cultivation surface stones should be collected and carted away. The end point of all this work should be a firm (but not compacted) and fine (but not dusty) seed bed.

Rotary cultivators seldom produce a satisfactory seed bed since, especially on heavy soils, they tend to form a 'pan' immediately beneath the cultivated soil. Also, rotary cultivation often results in damage to soil structure and in the top soil becoming 'fluffy' so that difficulty is experienced in producing the firm seed bed which is so desirable for turf establishment.

Surface Grading

Whether the final surface is horizontal or slightly sloping it is important to produce a playing surface which is smooth and free from water collecting hollows. Some form of 'blade-grading' is therefore necessary in the final stages of preparation. After soil amelioration further blade grading should be kept to the absolute minimum.

Soil Amelioration

For physical amelioration materials such as sand and peat can easily be worked into the top soil during the cultivations. The type and quantity of physical ameliorants required can be advised by an expert after testing samples.

Suitable soil tests can also give guidance on lime requirement (if any) and on suitable fertilizer treatment. If lime is needed it should be spread evenly and well cultivated into the top soil. There are very few circumstances where fertilizer pre-treatment is not worth while to help the new turf off to a good start and an average type of treatment is a granular fertilizer containing 10% N, 15% P_2O_5 and 10% K_2O at the rate of 35 to 70 g/m^2 (1 to 2 oz per sq yd) or 375 to 750 kg/ha (3 to 6 cwt per acre). Soil test results may suggest variations on this and on fine turf areas a balanced blend of powdered fertilizers may be used instead. The fertilizer (see FERTILIZERS) is raked or harrowed into the surface inch or two of soil preferably (but not essentially) a few days before sowing the grass seed.

81

Grass seed can be sown at various times of the year with some hope of success but spring and late summer are the main times. The latter is very much preferred in that it permits of soil preparation etc. under dry conditions and the seed is sown in a warm seed bed at a time when weeds offer less competition and when once the soil is moistened it rarely dries out again.

The seed (see GRASSES) is broadcast by hand, by seed fiddle or by seed barrow — drilling is usually unsatisfactory since it results in lines of grass seedlings which are slow to close up. The seed is thoroughly raked or chain harrowed into the surface and another stone picking operation carried out where necessary. In some circumstances rolling (e.g. with a Cambridge roller) may be advantageous. In urban areas it may be worth while using seed treated with bird repellent.

For large steep embankments, road verges etc. a relatively new process called hydraulic seeding is sometimes used. There is more than one version of this process which involves the use of large equipment to spread the seed in an aqueous spray which may contain fertilizers and even provide some material to cover the grass where it falls.

B. *Establishment from Turf*

Site preparation is generally as for seeding but, particularly since turfing is preferably an autumn job, a high proportion of quickly available nitrogen in the fertilizer is to be avoided. Quite often the old favourite pre-treatment of 35 to 70 g bone meal per m² (1 to 2 oz per sq yd) is sufficient on small areas but usually a more balanced fertilizer is appropriate (see FERTILIZERS).

Choice of Turf

Turf (see GRASSES) is usually purchased on the basis of samples. There are a few specialist turf growers but most turf on the market is semi-natural and finding good turf established in suitable soil is not easy. There is, therefore, much to be said for the special 'seedling' type of turf now commercially available and this should be handled according to suppliers' instructions.

Laying Ordinary Turf

The turf should be of convenient and uniform thickness – usually 31 mm (1¼ in) or 37 mm (1½ in) – and in pieces of convenient size, 300 mm (approx. 12 in) square for really accurate work but commonly 900 mm × 300 mm (approx. 3 ft × 1 ft) or 450 mm × 300 mm (18 in × 12 in). After laying the first row of turves the turf layer should work from boards laid over the turf – the prepared bed should not be spoiled. It is usually most convenient to lay the turf with a garden fork, each turf being packed close to its neighbours, working in straight lines. The turf should be laid with staggered joints so that when finished it resembles the brickwork in a wall. Any level adjustment necessary should be achieved by taking out or adding soil – *not* by beating.

On completion the area should be lightly rolled and top dressed with material appropriate to the area (sandy compost for bowling greens and golf greens, heavy soil for cricket tables).

FERTILIZERS

For healthy growth the grass plant requires an adequate supply of many mineral nutrients from the soil. Chief among these are the fertilizer elements – nitrogen, phosphorus and potassium. Grass may suffer from lack of these even though there are appreciable amounts in the soil since only part of the total content is in available form and it is the available amounts which are important. Apart from the available plant foods taken up by the grass (which may or may not be returned in cuttings) there are losses by leaching. Moreover some of the added supplies are fixed or made unavailable by certain chemical and biological processes. In order to maintain sufficient available amounts in the soil to maintain good growth it is therefore necessary to make good the various losses by the addition of fertilizers.

Nitrogen

Nitrogen is easily the most important nutrient. It encourages growth generally and is the nutrient removed in largest quantities by the grass; consequently it is the fertilizer element required in largest quantities. The form in which nitrogen is applied can have effects reaching far beyond those of simple nitrogen supply to plants. It has been found in trials that different fertilizers with equivalent amounts of nitrogen affect in different ways such turf properties as weed and worm populations, drought resistance, types of grass and hardness of turf.

Sulphate of ammonia (21% N) has been found to be the most satisfactory individual nitrogen fertilizer *if used properly.* Prolonged exclusive use can lead to over-acidity, which causes thinning out of the sward and increase in fibre, in which case a corrective dressing of lime may be needed. In general sulphate of ammonia forms the basis of any fertilizer programme for turf areas.

For fine turf areas it is often desirable to supply a proportion of the nitrogen in the form of an organic fertilizer such as dried blood (12 or 13% N) or hoof and horn meal (12 or 13% N).Dried blood is a quick acting fertilizer but hoof and horn meal is much slower. Used alone these tend to have detrimental effects but do increase drought resistance. A balanced supply of nitrogen in the forms of sulphate of ammonia and organic fertilizers, the proportions varying according to the soil, will help to maintain steady growth, to keep the soil slightly acid and to hold down weed and worm populations without causing over-acidity too quickly.

Other nitrogenous fertilizers are available and some find use on sports turf under special conditions. Nitro-chalk (25% N) for example, a mixture of ammonium nitrate and lime, is often useful on areas that have become over-acid but where the application of lime as such is not desirable or practicable. If used regularly as the main source of nitrogen however nitro-chalk can have a detrimental effect on the quality of the turf. Among other nitrogen fertilizers available are:- nitrate of soda (16% N), urea (45% N), ammonium nitrate (35% N) etc., all of which have their place occasionally.

There has long been a requirement for good 'slow-release' nitrogen fertilizers. This has in the past been met to some extent by the use of organic materials but in recent years new purpose-made slow-release nitrogenous fertilizers have come on the market in proprietary form. These have received some acceptance but there may be better ones to come!

Three different fertilizer distributors.

Phosphorus

Phosphorus is less important than nitrogen but is still needed. Phosphorus is claimed to encourage root growth, especially if used in conjunction with nitrogen, but it tends to encourage clovers if used alone or with insufficient nitrogen. The most common phosphatic fertilizers used on turf are superphosphate (available in both powder and granular form) and finely ground bone meal. In superphosphate (16 to 21% P_2O_5) almost all the phosphate is soluble and quickly available (although because of reaction with the soil it is not readily leached away). Bone meal (2 to 4% N and 20 to 30% P_2O_5) is almost insoluble in water and therefore slower acting.

Ground mineral phosphate (25 to 40% P_2O_5) and basic slag (8 to 18% P_2O_5) are sometimes (though rarely) used; both are alkaline materials supplying slow acting phosphate and they are sometimes of value on areas like golf fairways which are deficient in phosphate and have become over-acid as well.

Potassium

Potassium is the least important of the three major nutrients as far as turf grasses are concerned. In plants one of its main functions is to assist development of seeds and fruits and, as most turf grasses are not allowed to produce seeds, potassium requirements are relatively low. Some potassium is usually applied as part of a balanced fertilizer programme because it is needed by the plant for other functions; it also increases drought resistance and may affect disease resistance. The usual forms applied are sulphate of potash (48 or 50% K_2O) and chloride (muriate) of potash (60% K_2O). The sulphate is probably the most commonly used because because it is easier to store etc.

Organic Fertilizers

In addition to dried blood, hoof and horn meal and bone meal there are various other organic materials which can be used in fertilizer mixtures for turf. These include fish meal, blood and bone meal and various waste products of plant or animal origin any of which might be used in proprietary fertilizer formulations. Organic fertilizers are useful constituents of fine turf mixtures when balanced suitably with inorganics – they have the effect of spreading out the growth response and they help drought resistance. Over-use of organics tends to produce a soft turf liable to invasion by earthworms, weeds and disease.

Fertilizer Analysis

When a fertilizer is sold the seller should supply analytical details of its composition in terms of nitrogen, phosphate and potash. The analysis is expressed in terms of N (nitrogen), P_2O_5 (phosphoric acid) and K_2O (potash). The percentages do not add up to a total of 100% because each of the plant foods is in chemically combined form (and, of course, fertilizers do not have to be absolutely pure).

Lime/Fertilizer Relationships

It is important to bear in mind that the soil reaction (alkalinity/acidity) governs the efficiency of the fertilizer applied. An approximately neutral reaction is usually best (possibility slightly acid for fine turf); if the soil is allowed to become *too* acid the response of the grass to most types of fertilizer will be poor. On the other hand if the soil becomes too alkaline there may be trouble from worms, weeds and disease. It is desirable in most circumstances to use fertilizers which are acid or neutral in character, dressing the turf with ground carbonate of lime if the pH drops too low.

Effects of cutting disposal on fertilizer requirement

When fine turf areas are mown cuttings are usually removed, taking with them their content of mineral nutrients. On more extensive turf areas cuttings are usually allowed to fly and their mineral content is thus returned to the soil when they decompose. The former areas therefore need more fertilizer than the latter.

Solid or liquid fertilizers

Since sprayers and good watering systems are increasingly available there is a decided interest in the possibilities of fertilizer application in solution. Unfortunately this has severe limitations and solid applications are preferred. With liquid application the types of fertilizer which can be used are limited by the need for full solubility. Even the best of watering systems fall far short of the uniformity of distribution required for fertilizer while if appreciable amounts of fertilizer are sprayed on to the turf there is a definite scorch risk.

Fertilizers for fine turf

A well-balanced fertilizer contains suitable proportions of the main plant foods; nitrogen, phosphate and potash. In some cases a little sulphate of iron in the calcined form is included as a 'turf conditioner'. For fine turf as on greens, tennis courts, lawns and so forth 'straight' fertilizers like sulphate of ammonia, dried blood, superphosphate, bone meal and sulphate of potash (plus sulphate of iron) may be mixed to a formula which suits the soil and the turf, and bulked out with a carrier of screened sandy compost or top soil to ensure even distribution.

A typical spring fertilizer might, for instance, be made up as follows:

	per 100 m²	OR per 100 sq yd
sulphate of ammonia (21% N)	1.5 kg	3 lb
dried blood (12·5% N	0.5 kg	1 lb
powdered superphosphate (20% P₂O₅)	2.0 kg	4 lb
fine bone meal (4% N 20% P₂O₅)	0.5 kg	1 lb
sulphate of potash (50% K₂O)	0.5 kg	1 lb
calcined sulphate of iron (say 22% Fe)	0.5 kg	1 lb
with		
screened compost or soil	14.0 kg	28 lb

Leaving out the carrier the analysis of the fertilizer is:

$$7.2\% \text{ N}$$
$$9.1\% \text{ P}_2\text{O}_5$$
$$4.5\% \text{ K}_2\text{O}$$
$$2.0\% \text{ Fe}$$

Satisfactory mixing of fertilizers is a decidely testing operation. If the fertilizer constituents are mixed together before adding the carrier of compost or soil they will 'set' together unless used immediately despite the conditioning influence of the organics. If this happens the mix should be left to mature for eight or ten weeks and then broken up and screened (not too easy an operation), after which it should not go hard again unless it gets damp. When the mixture is diluted with the carrier immediately or when the whole end product of fertilizer plus carrier is produced in one operation just prior to use there should be no difficulty with setting. In either case actual mixing of the various materials can be achieved by spreading each one out in successive layers to make a flat (not conical) heap and then turning/mixing at least five times before finally passing through a fine screen.

NOTE. All fertilizers are not necessarily compatible with each other in mixtures. The ones mentioned *are* compatible – others might not be.

Because of the inconvenience of making up mixtures many people prefer to buy proprietary products despite possible extra cost and purchase a commercial spring/summer fertilizer instead of the above kind of mixture.

For a lawn a single complete fertilizer dressing in the spring is usually ample. For fine sports turf (golf greens, tennis courts, cricket squares and bowling greens) it is often necessary to give further dressings, mainly nitrogenous, during the growing season at intervals of four to eight weeks as judged necessary. A suitable summer dressing could be made up of the first two items of the spring dressing plus the carrier of screened compost or soil, e.g.:

	per 100 m²	**OR** per 100 sq yd
sulphate of ammonia	1·5 kg	3 lb
dried blood	0·5 kg	1 lb
with		
screened compost or soil	14·0 kg	28 lb

Here again a proprietary fertilizer could be used instead if preferred.

It is important to ensure sufficient but not excessive growth in the autumn months and to this end a last summer fertilizer dressing (say, at the end of August) is particularly necessary. According to circumstances, it may be a repeat of the summer nitrogenous fertilizer as above or possibly a complete fertilizer as in spring or a compromise between them.

If using proprietary products it is wise to consider the maker's approach – e.g. he may provide a particular fertilizer which is so balanced as to be suitable for repeated use during the whole of the summer.

Some groundsmen and greenkeepers are convinced of the value of autumn/winter feeds although on turf treated generally as above there is some doubt as to their necessity.

Those using autumn/winter fertilizers usually aim to give a complete fertilizer which is relatively low in nitrogen. This has frequently been achieved by say, for example, a mixture of:

7 parts bone meal (say 4% N and 20% P_2O_5)
3 parts sulphate of potash (say 50% K_2O)

which gives an analysis of 2.8% N, 14% P_2O_5 and 15% K_2O and might be used at 70 g/m² (2 oz. per sq yd). Since phosphate and potash are not readily lost from most soils there may be little need to put extra dressings on in the period of low growth so that the main value of this mixture probably lies in the small amount of slow acting nitrogen. Indeed in the past many bowling green keepers gave their bowling greens an annual winter dressing of bone meal alone at 70 g/m² (2 oz per sq yd) with the result that the soil became very high indeed in phosphate. Proprietary autumn/winter fertilizers no doubt vary in their composition but they are usually complete fertilizers low in nitrogen.

Suitable fertilizer programmes vary enormously in fact from sports ground to sports ground and from golf course to golf course depending on the needs of the particular turf and soil and the demands made upon them by the different sets of players.

Fertilizers for the more coarse types of turf

For the somewhat coarser type of turf like that on winter playing pitches, racecourses, cricket outfields and golf fairways, proprietary granular fertilizers containing suitable proportions of the main plant foods (e.g. 10% N,15% P_2O_5, 10% K_2O or 20% N, 10% P_2O_5, 10% K_2O) have been widely used in recent years and there is no need to go in for special mixes of powered fertilizers as a rule. A suitable rate might be 375 kg/ha (3 cwt. per acre) and no carrier is required for granular fertilizers.

One dressing of fertilizer in the spring is enough for the average football, rugby and hockey pitch although the soccer and rugby pitches used by big professional clubs will need perhaps three or more dressings, suitably spaced out through the growing season. Cricket outfields may benefit from a dressing perhaps every other spring while most golf fairways will need still less fertilizer. For racecourses an annual spring dressing of complete granular fertilizer is usually sufficient.

Fertilizer application

It is very important that all fertilizers, of whatever sort they are, be applied as evenly as possible and, if practicable, during broken weather when there is rain to wash them in. On fine turf, at least, if no rain falls within one or two days then the fertilizer should be watered in.

Excessive concentrations of certain fertilizers caused by uneven application can scorch the grass and actually cause bare

90

places. Uneven application, in any case, results in uneven colour and growth and in a patchy playing surface.

The virtues of spreading by hand

For relatively small sports turf areas like golf greens there is no doubt that there is nothing to beat hand application where there is time and skilled labour available for the job. The fertilizer (plus carrier) is divided in two, and the two halves carefully spread by hand from a hopper in two directions at right angles to each other. Remarkable evenness and accuracy may thus be achieved. Otherwise it is a question of choosing one of the best of the various mechanical distributors on the market and using it intelligently.

For larger areas a machine is almost essential, of course. If a distributor of the 'spinner' type is to be used it should be checked to make sure that it produces a sufficiently even distribution pattern.

Timing of Fertilizer application

Timing is important. If the right fertilizer is applied at the wrong time or under the wrong conditions the effects can be disappointing to say the least. In spring it is important not to apply too early. There is often a 'false spring' quite early in the year followed by a return to wintry conditions; if nitrogen fertilizer is applied during the false spring there will be new growth which may be much damaged by subsequent frost.

In summer, dressings of nitrogen should not be applied during periods of dry weather unless water is available, otherwise severe scorch can occur.

In the late summer the final nitrogen dressing should not be too late, possibly not after the end of August, otherwise the lush growth in the autumn can lay the turf open to damage in severe weather and to attacks of fungal diseases such as fusarium. On the other hand it is important to encourage some growth to continue well into the autumn.

Fertilizer to use when establishing new turf areas

The precise composition of the fertilizer to use when establishing new turf areas may depend on soil tests but the information below covers average circumstances.

A granular fertilizer containing 10% N, 15% P_2O_5 and 10% K_2O used at 375–750 kg/ha (3–6 cwt. per acre) which is approximately the same as 35–70 g/m² (1–2 oz. per sq yd is suitable as a pre-seeding fertilizer for most kinds of turf. When sowing down important fine turf areas a powder mixture on the following lines may be preferred:

	per 100 m²	OR per 100 sq. yd.
sulphate of ammonia	1.5 kg	3 lb
dried blood	0.5 kg	1 lb
powdered superphosphate	3.0 kg	6 lb
fine bone meal	1.0 kg	2 lb
sulphate of potash	0.5 kg	1 lb

It is best if the fertilizer (of whatever kind) can be applied and raked or harrowed in to the surface soil about a week before grass seed is sown.

Turf is preferably laid in the late autumn when plentiful nitrogen may be detrimental and so the fertilizer used should be lower in nitrogen than those described above. On small areas there is much to be said for the convenience of applying simply a dressing of phosphatic fertilizer, e.g. superphosphate or bone meal or a 50/50 mixture of the two at up to 70 g/m² (2 oz per sq yd). If potash is considered advisable treatment might be:

9 parts bone meal
1 part sulphate of potash

at 70 g/m² (2 oz per sq yd). For turf laid during the growing months of the year a proportion of nitrogenous fertilizer may be advantageous as in the following mixture which is intended for use at 70 g/m² (2 oz per sq yd):

	per 100 m²	OR per 100 sq yd
sulphate of ammonia	0.5 kg	1 lb
fine hoof and horn meal	0.5 kg	1 lb
powdered superphosphate	3.0 kg	6 lb
fine bone meal	1.0 kg	2 lb
sulphate of potash	1.0 kg	2 lb

Ready prepared proprietary fertilizers may, of course, be used if desired for either pre-seeding or pre-turfing treatment.

92

FIBRE — EXCESS AND CONTROL

Turf which contains fine-leaved species of grass, particularly fine turf, in course of time tends to build up an excessive layer of fibrous material (sometimes termed mat or thatch) at the surface. This layer is formed from a variable mixture of dead plant material in various stages of decay and living (possibly moribund) stems and roots. The fibre lies beneath the green aerial growth but mainly above the soil into which it may be very little incorporated. The layer restricts moisture penetration and fibrous turf has poor drought resistance. On the other hand in wet weather the turf lies soft and wet because of this condition while disease attack may be frequent. The soft fibrous top provides a poor playing surface and takes the imprint of players' footwear; the growth of the grass is weak and very often moss begins to colonize the least vigorous parts of the turf.

Causes Not Fully Comprehended

The reasons for excessive surface fibre development — which is to be seen chiefly on golf greens and bowling greens but also on other types of sports turf including golf fairways — are not yet completely understood. It is thought that there are several contributing factors.

In quite a lot of cases inadequate drainage seems to be an important factor. When the soil is waterlogged for at least part of the year and consequently short of air, roots will not go down into it and so they stay near the surface and the turf (with the aid of fertilizer) more or less grows on itself and a fibrous surface layer is produced. This in turn holds water. Thus we are frequently in the position of pondering whether the fibre is caused by wetness or the wetness by fibre!

Too generous watering (only too easy with modern automatic systems) also produces a sodden, airless condition ideal for the development of peaty fibre. Over-watering encourages fibre, the increased depth of fibre soaks up still more water and the fault is again progressive.

93

Some research workers believe that the increased use of fungicides is killing off the useful fungi which normally would be decomposing the dead grass.

Turf which is over-acid builds up excess fibre; this has been common knowledge for a long time in turf management circles and is no new discovery. The acid, airless, wet peat bogs on the Pennine moors and elsewhere are, in fact, an extension of the condition we find on some golf greens.

Top dressings with a high proportion of soft, undecomposed organic matter, peat, for example, or leaf mould, will obviously aggravate the condition and so will insufficient aeration and lack of scarification.

Prevention

Good management, with particular attention to the points noted – moisture control and acidity control – and with routine scarification regularly and thoroughly carried out should prevent the formation of a mat or thatch layer sufficient to be detrimental.

Elimination

If a thick wad of fibre already exists then obviously the first thing is to remove the possible causes as far as they are known. Improvement of drainage may involve new pipe drains, slit drainage, more aeration or combinations of these. Hollow tining in the autumn helps surplus water away, lets air into the fibrous mat (thus encouraging decomposition of dead material) and also physically removes some of the fibre. Close hollow tining followed up by a top dressing with good sandy compost brings about a considerable improvement in the firmness of soft matted turf.

Lime can be used to correct over-acidity if soil tests show this to be present – it is a mistake to assume that excessively fibrous turf automatically needs lime.

There have been trials with various additives with a view to assisting in the breakdown of the fibre layer but none have proved very efficient so far and the only practical approach to removal of excess fibre from existing turf is severe scarification (see SCARIFICATION) at appropriate times of the year.

The Surgical Approach

In severe cases elimination of excessive fibre by surface methods is likely to take many years and in such circumstances it may well be worth while to lift the turf thinly leaving most of the fibre behind and then re-lay after suitable cultivations etc.

GOLF COURSES

The Playing Surfaces

Golf course management provides a very wide range of interest for the greenkeeper. The greens need to be of high quality fine turf providing smooth, fast and predictable putting surfaces which nevertheless will hold a pitch shot; they have much in common with bowling greens. Teeing grounds must provide a firm level surface of considerable durability and, therefore, have something in common with cricket tables and tennis courts. The fairways are required to provide a good run for the ball and a good lie ready for the next shot but too much growth makes for unnecessary mowing – the requirements are similar to those of a cricket outfield. In addition to the above the greenkeeper's responsibilities also include green approaches and surrounds, grassy banks, the rough, bunkers and, as often as possible, a turf nursery to provide replacement turf for greens and tees. It must be remembered also that the greenkeeper has the problems conferred by the fact that golf is an all the year round game and not just a summer game like the others mentioned. This means, amongst other things, that all aspects of drainage are particularly important on a golf course. The wide range of work to be done means competition for staff at critical periods so that the greenkeeper needs to be a good organiser.

Although golf is played all the year round the main playing season is undoubtedly the summer so that a convenient time to consider as the start of the greenkeeping year is late summer or early autumn when all areas are likely to be showing the effects of several months' heavy use.

GREENS

Autumn

Play goes on all through the winter and it is important to maintain growth well into the autumn so that fertilizer treatment needs some consideration. It is, however, usually wise to give very little fertilizer (see FERTILIZER) after a good dressing at about the end of August but there is something to be said for later dressings in some circumstances.

Many golf greens throughout the country suffer from an excess of fibrous growth at the surface – a layer of mat or thatch which consists of a mixture of living, moribund and dead stems etc. of the herbage. *Early* autumn is a good time to make a thorough attack on this problem with a scarifier. At this time most of the particularly important golf is finished but there is still time for growth to restore the surface which may be damaged during the severe scarification. This is normally done with one of the mechanical scarifiers or 'vertical cutters' which are proving so popular and useful. If the surface is damaged by the scarification a little over-seeding may be necessary but normally there is not much renovation work to do on golf greens.

Aeration in some form is becoming increasingly important because increased play, particularly in the winter, leads to increased compaction. Some form of aeration is therefore necessary and this may well take the form of spiking or slitting by machine. Sometimes (but not too frequently) hollow tine or spoon tine aeration is advisable to ease the compression, assist aeration and moisture penetration and increase root development. Top dressing with sandy compost, preferably made on the course from natural materials, used to be the stand-by of the greenkeepers of yester-year, went out of favour somewhat at one time but nowadays is being relied upon more and more to maintain greens in first-class condition despite heavy usage. This should be applied before growth ceases.

During the autumn months regular switching or brushing is desirable to disperse the dew and any worm casts which may be produced. Incidentally, autumn is a good time for earthworm control if this is necessary. There is still quite a lot of growth but mowing needs doing progressively less frequently as the cold weather approaches. It is wise to cut as regularly as necessary but

96

Using powered drag mats to work compost into a golf green.

to gradually raise the height of cut to about 8 mm (5/16 in).

Final preparations should be given to the sites maintained for 'winter' greens, these being preferably not on the approaches (which are already hard worn) but to the side somewhere.

Winter

During the winter regular switching and brushing is necessary, possibly daily, and occasional mowing at the increased height of cut is usually wanted as well. Holes should be changed particularly frequently in the winter because of the damage which occurs immediately around the hole and, despite the possible unpopularity of the move, serious consideration should be given to the use in bad weather of ready-prepared winter greens (see WINTER USE OF GOLF GREENS) so as to preserve the main ones and ensure that they are in good condition for the following summer season. In winter particularly, but also at other times of the year, plug marks should regularly be eased up by means of a hand weeding fork and repaired as necessary.

Spring

It may sometimes be necessary to give a light roll to firm up any upheaval which has resulted from a severe winter and very frequently further aeration with slit or solid tines is beneficial. Particularly if the greens have been heavily used over the winter a light dressing of sandy compost will help to restore the surfaces for the summer. Switching or brushing the surface is still almost a daily requirement. As growth increases the frequency of mowing has to be increased and the cutters gradually lowered to the summer height of cut though this should not be reached too quickly.

Application of the spring fertilizer is a matter for careful timing. If it is put on too early the grass can suffer from late frosts whilst if it is put on too late the greens do not reach their summer quality until later than is necessary. A good general fertilizer is usually most appropriate and distribution must be to a high standard. As growth gets away under the influence of fertilizer a very good opportunity is presented for selective weedkilling if this is necessary.

Summer

The main job here is regular mowing, e.g. three times a week at a height of cut of 5 mm (3/16 in), the cuttings being boxed off as always. To get a good finish from the mowing and to restrict the formation of unwanted fibrous material at the surface regular light scarification of some kind should be carried out. Late spring or early summer is usually the best time for selective weedkilling and it is often wise to time things so that the weedkiller can be applied about a fortnight after a dressing of fertilizer. During the summer, fertilizer treatment, particularly of a nitrogenous nature, may be needed every month or so with particular emphasis on a good dressing at the end of August to carry through the autumn months. Even in the summer it is wise not to leave holes in the same place too long and this matter should receive constant attention.

98

There are many people who would prefer not to water golf greens in that the finer grasses stand drought better than the unwanted grasses such as annual meadow-grass, but golfers' requirements for 'holding' greens and for good looking turf seem to make it necessary for watering even in moderate drought. If water is to be used at all it is important to get it on early enough (i.e. before the grass is taking harm) and to give sufficient to maintain the soil moisture content to full root depth. Shallow spiking or pricking helps water penetration in difficult circumstances.

Approaches

These should be maintained generally as for the greens but frequently they need more aeration than the actual greens.

TEEING GROUNDS

Autumn

Attention should be given to the winter tees where these are available so as to prepare them for bringing into play, say during October. The main tees should have had fertilizer but if they have not had any for some time it may not be too late to promote growth with a general fertilizer.

The important work is aeration, renovation (by seed or turf as appropriate) and top dressing with sandy compost or with soil as seems the most appropriate for any given tee. For areas which are really badly damaged, turf is often used for repairs, the turf being obtained from a turf nursery or from selected areas of fairways. Turfing can be carried out later in the year than can seeding but wet weather may interfere with the thorough preparation of the site.

Mowing should continue as required, although the cutter should be raised a little. It is often necessary to make special efforts to keep tree-surrounded tees clear of leaves which would smother the grass and encourage disease.

Winter

During the winter keeping clear of leaves and occasional spiking are the main operations although, if renovation was not completed or has failed, further renovating by turfing can still be done. Even during the winter occasional mowing is required during mild weather.

Spring

Further aeration and light scarification are usually desirable. Fertilizer treatment may be with a mixed fertilizer such as used for the greens or in some circumstances a granular complete fertilizer may be appropriate. Further top dressing may also be required. Mowing should gradually increase in frequency, with the height of cut progressively dropped to the summer height of 6–13 mm (¼–½ in). It is important now and at all times to move tee markers frequently to spread wear.

Winter tees are frequently in very bad condition when spring arrives and therefore in need of a lot of attention. Any grass remaining should be encouraged by a good dressing of granular fertilizer. The tees should then be thoroughly aerated and a seed bed prepared to receive grass seed which is well raked in. There is much to be said for including an appreciable proportion of a good perennial ryegrass in the seeds mixture used in repairing winter tees.

Summer

As with all grass areas regular frequent mowing to 6–12.5 mm (¼–½ in), e.g. twice a week, is the order of the day and it helps to keep firm hard-wearing tees if the cuttings are boxed off. Fertilizer may be required every time the greens get fertilizer though tees do not usually need quite as much. It is important, however, to make sure that they get some fertilizer in the late summer or early autumn to keep growth going during the autumn months. If selective weedkilling is required it should preferably come about a fortnight after any of the fertilizer dressings during the spring and summer. Where watering facilities are available watering should not be forgotten in dry weather – not all the

Leaf sweeping on a golf course.

attention should be given to the greens. Moving tee markers and carrying out running repairs should receive constant attention.

FAIRWAYS

Autumn

Most fairways benefit from scarification by means of chain harrows or by means of some of the modern equipment which has been produced for the purpose. A good spiking is also usually beneficial, particularly on heavy land where spiking should be repeated at intervals. Less frequent mowing will be required as the season advances and the cutters can with advantage be raised a little. On many courses leaves are a problem and some form of clearance is necessary at intervals.

Golf fairways as a whole seldom need renovation but there are areas subject to particular wear, e.g. by caddy carts, which have to receive attention from time to time, generally on the same lines as the tees.

Winter

Occasional mowing (not too short) is still required when there is marked growth in mild weather and, particularly on heavy land, regular spiking when soil conditions permit.

Spring

More aeration should be given as appropriate and usually further scarification early in the spring. The question of fertilizers for fairways has been the subject of some argument. In the past not much fertilizer was given but many old established clubs are now finding that at least one dressing a year is necessary and frequently a granular fertilizer containing 10–15–10 is appropriate at 250–375 kg/ha (2–3 cwt per acre). Quite clearly over-feeding is to be avoided. More frequent mowing becomes necessary as the season advances and, of course, the cutters can be gradually lowered to their summer level.

Summer

The main operation here is regular mowing at 12.5–18 mm (½–¾ in) generally once per week and avoidance of excessive feeding is of considerable advantage in reducing the amount of mowing necessary. If selective weedkilling is required it should be carried out during periods when there is good growth so that the grass is likely to fill in quickly any spaces left by dying weeds. Some running repairs will be required, especially divoting.

The Rough

Usually the aim here is merely to maintain reasonable tidiness and to minimise the loss of expensive balls. This commonly means simply occasional cutting with a gang mower or with some kind of rotary cutter. Lime and fertilizer are very rarely given, if ever, but on some old golf courses *some* treatment may be necessary from time to time over the years.

Turf Nursery

As far as possible maintenance of the turf in the nursery should be similar to that of the turf areas for which the turf is intended.

There should be some turf for tees and some for greens, say 400 m² (500 sq yds) of each and the nursery site should preferably be chosen to facilitate regular maintenance as much as possible. Nursery turf is useful for routine renovation; it is also useful for the replacement of patches of turf infested with weed grasses such as Yorkshire fog and for replacing turf damaged by accident or by vandals.

Bunkers

Bunker maintenance is a much more costly item than most golfers realise. Routine work consists mainly of maintaining the presence of sand to the right thickness in the right places and keeping the surfaces smooth. Replacement supplies of the right kind of sand (not too abrasive but resistant to wind erosion) ought to be kept on hand. There is no recognised British specification for bunker sand but in the U.S.A. the accepted specification covers sands with particles in the range 0.25 mm–1.0 mm. Where possible a good sand of this type should be used. Raking of the sand in the bunkers should be a daily job if possible so as to keep the sand sufficiently loose, to regulate thickness, to draw sand up the bunker faces and to leave the surface smooth. With regular raking there should be little trouble from weed invasion but if a weed problem does arise care should be taken in any use of herbicide to avoid risk to adjacent turf from contaminated sand splash. Suitable materials to use are non-residual types which include paraquat, diquat and possibly glyphosate (SEE WEEDKILLERS FOR NON-GRASS SURFACES).

Cutting the fringes of the 'run-up', and of the lips and banks of bunkers is important if they are to serve their intended purpose and provide fair conditions for play. This trimming is commonly done at approximately fortnightly intervals.

General Smartness

Flags and flag poles, tee markers, distance posts, etc. kept in showroom condition add much to the golfer's pleasure and to his appreciation of the greenkeeper's efforts.

GRASSES

I. CHOOSING GRASSES FOR TURF USE

Species and Cultivars

Choice of grass depends on the use to which turf is to be put. The chosen grass needs to be persistent at the required height of cut and under the wear conditions imposed as well as having characteristics suitable for the purpose required, e.g. colour, texture for playing surface, etc. Disease resistance is also important.

For mowing at 5 mm (3/16 in) or less, e.g. on fine lawns, golf greens, bowling greens, first class cricket tables and tennis courts, the most important grasses are bents *(Agrostis* spp.). Creeping bent is usually sown by itself but browntop is more commonly used in mixture with red fescue.

Browntop bent *(Agrostis tenuis)* is the main bent in the U.K. There are two main types currently marketed:

1. The cultivar 'Highland' from Oregon, previously known as 'Oregon' browntop. (This may, strictly, be a different species, *Agrostis castellana*.)
2. The more expensive Dutch cultivars such as 'Bardot', 'Holfior' and 'Tracenta'.

The latter are finer-leaved, denser, lower growing and less prone to corticium than 'Highland' but not as green in winter. In summer, appearance depends largely on age of sward, amount of thatch and watering: the Dutch cultivars are likely to be more attractive than 'Highland' unless they develop too much thatch or there is severe drought.

Creeping bent *(Agrostis stolonifera)* is widely used in the U.S.A. and Mediterranean countries, where it has generally been established vegetatively. There is, however, increasing use of cultivars of which seed is available, e.g. 'Penncross', 'Prominent' and 'Smaragd'. 'Penncross' is a good cultivar, blue-green and with potentially good summer appearance if kept watered and free of thatch, though less attractive in winter. 'Prominent' and 'Smaragd' are lighter green than 'Penncross'. Creeping bents need a higher pH than does browntop bent and the stolons tend to produce 'nap' giving a biased playing surface.

104

Velvet bent (*Agrostis canina* ssp. *canina*) is seldom used at present in Britain, although it is finer-leaved than browntop. The cultivar 'Kingstown' from the U.S.A., though currently unobtainable commercially in the U.K., is outstanding. It is very fine-leaved, dense and attractive in summer, even in drought, though less attractive in winter: it is liable to problems of fibre accumulation and accompanying diseases as well as producing a nap.

Red fescue (*Festuca rubra*) is divided into three sub-species or groups:–

(i) Chewings fescue (*F. rubra* ssp. *commutata*). Fine-leaved; relatively low-growing; not spreading (no rhizomes); relatively disease resistant. Good cultivars (e.g. 'Barfalla', 'Famosa', 'Highlight', 'Koket', 'Waldorf') tolerate mowing at 5 mm (3/16 in) and choice partly depends on the season when colour is required, e.g. 'Highlight' is best from autumn to early spring, 'Waldorf' best in summer. 'Waldorf' produces an outstandingly close dense turf. 'Cascade' ('Oregon' Chewings) is appreciably poorer than the best cultivars in persistence, sward quality and disease resistance.

(ii) Slender creeping red fescue (*F. rubra* ssp. *litoralis*, etc.) 42 chromosomes: fine-leaved and low-growing; only short or slender rhizomes; some cultivars susceptible to corticium and dollar spot, especially the 'sea-marsh' type. 'Dawson' tolerates mowing at 5 mm (3/16 in) fairly well, establishes vigorously and has good dark green colour if there is no disease. 'Aberystwyth S.59' is tolerant of fairly close mowing, e.g. 10 mm (3/8 in), but not of very close mowing, and grows strongly in winter.

(iii) Strong creeping red fescue (*F. rubra* ssp. *rubra*). 56 chromosomes: coarser darker leaves and stronger rhizomes than slender creeping red fescue; relatively tall-growing; susceptible to corticium, particularly when mown close. Some of the Dutch cultivars – 'Agio', 'Bargena', 'Novorubra' and 'Ruby' – approach 'Aberystwyth S.59' in density under fairly close mowing. Danish cultivars have quite good winter colour, but are rather susceptible to disease. Canadian cultivars – e.g. 'Boreal' – have rather poor winter colour. There appears to be relatively little difference within this whole group when turf is mown at or above 20 mm (3/4 in).

105

The finest leaved fescues are hard fescue *(F. longifolia)*, sheep's fescue *(F. ovina)* and fine-leaved sheep's fescue *(F. tenuifolia)*. They are better adapted than red fescue to acid, infertile or very dry conditions. They may be useful for semi-natural grassland, because of short growth that needs less cutting, but they do not establish vigorously. They are not suitable for very fine turf, but some cultivars, e.g. 'Biljart' hard fescue, can look very attractive when mown at 20–25 mm (¾ –1 in). Sheep's fescue and fine-leaved sheep's fescue tolerate close mowing but tend to grow in unattractive whorls and are prone to corticium.

Smooth-stalked meadow-grass *(Poa pratensis)* is slow in establishing but can be tough and hard wearing with good recovery if mown not lower than 20 mm (¾ in). Good cultivars, if well established, can tolerate 12.5 mm (½ in) for at least a year, but need careful management (moderate, not excessive, nitrogen and a rest from close mowing some time in the growing season) if they are not to thin out over a period of years. The rhizomes give good recovery from wear and some drought tolerance. Smooth-stalked meadow-grass does not like wet soils or low pH. Susceptibility to melting-out disease is a serious disadvantage, although some cultivars are more resistant than others. Good broad-leaved cultivars available at present in the U.K. for football fields, etc. include 'Parade', 'Monopoly', 'Baron' and 'Sydsport'. The last two may show poor winter colour. 'Fylking' is also a good cultivar but with finer leaves and more suited to blend with fescue/bent than the others.

Rough-stalked meadow-grass *(Poa trivialis)* may be substituted for smooth-stalked in wet situations which it tolerates better, and its establishment is faster. It is, however, less tolerant of wear and normally not worth using. There is some seed of named cultivars available from Denmark.

There are two species of timothy – the large-leaved *(Phleum pratense)* and the small-leaved *(P. bertolonii)*. Both are hard-wearing; having no rhizomes they do not repair damage like smooth-stalked meadow-grass but they establish more easily, have no serious disease problem and tolerate wet heavy soils. Good cultivars of the large-leaved timothy (e.g. 'Pastremo' or 'Aberystwyth S.48') tolerate cutting at 20 mm (¾ in). The size of leaf and blue-green colour are disadvantages. The small-leaved species (e.g. 'Aberystwyth S.50') is finer-leaved and tolerates closer cutting; it makes good hard-wearing turf with fescue and bent mown at 12.5 mm (½ in).

Crested dogstail *(Cynosurus cristatus)* is of uncertain value. In some European countries it is considered a tough and quite persistent grass when mown at 12.5 mm (½ in) or more, but it has recently shown no special value in this respect in trials in the U.K. It is still used to some extent in fine turf mixtures but does not blend with red fescue and bent and in most situations only scattered plants persist under close cutting. Most seed is from New Zealand and now bears the cultivar name 'Southlands'.

For football fields and comparable turf for general purposes (including golf fairways, school playing fields, parks, etc.) perennial ryegrass *(Lolium perenne)* is quick to establish, vigorous in growth and good cultivars persist well under heavy wear provided the height of cut is not less than 20 mm (¾ in) and preferably a little higher. Cultivars bred for sports turf (e.g. 'Manhattan', 'Sprinter') are very hard-wearing, but under mowing without wear can show corticium and look perhaps less attractive than some cultivars originally bred for agriculture which are nevertheless very good for intensive turf use, e.g. 'Pelo', 'Melle', 'Barenza', 'Aberystwyth S.23' and 'Lamora'. 'Grandstand' is another good cultivar.

Annual meadow-grass *(Poa annua)* is often regarded as a weed grass, particularly in fine or ornamental turf, but it is hard-wearing and tolerant of close mowing, able to replace itself by seeding at all heights of cut and to grow all the year round even on compacted soils. Susceptibility to fusarium, poor colour in drought and winter, and presence of seed heads are the main drawbacks, but it also kicks out fairly readily in some circumstances. Such seed as is available commercially is of a type less dense and persistent than naturally selected types, which are best 'sown' by spreading cuttings.

Seeds Mixtures

The seeds mixture for a playing surface should provide the best possible balance of species and cultivars to withstand hard wear and other conditions of stress and give an acceptable playing quality and appearance. At present, there is not enough evidence from nation-wide trials to give a list of recommended mixtures and the mixtures in the table below are only for general guidance.

Under recent legislation, certified seed of named cultivars is the only category available for general use in certain species including perennial ryegrass, timothy, smooth-stalked meadow-grass and red fescue. In other species, including bents, one may be able to buy either certified seed of named cultivars (the normally preferable choice) or the lower grade of commercial seed, which may carry a cultivar name though cultivar reliability is not assured. Therefore the phrase 'certified seed' is not strictly needed for every component of a mixture, though it is probably wise – at least for the present – to include it throughout.

Where there are several cultivars of equal merit it is probably worth giving two or three alternatives when ordering. Sometimes, however, it may be necessary to stipulate one particular cultivar.

(a) Mixtures for intensive use

Some appropriate types of mixture are shown opposite: they are on the whole harder-wearing towards the right-hand side of the Table.

The situations in which the mixtures could be used are as follows:

(a) Very fine turf mown at 5 mm (3/16 in) e.g. bowling greens, golf greens, putting greens, croquet lawns, cricket tables, tennis courts.

Season of turf use may influence choice of cultivar. For cricket tables, some groundsmen include crested dogstail or good perennial ryegrass in the mixture.

(b) Fine turf mown at 10 mm (3/8 in) or less, e.g. some hockey pitches, golf tees, tennis courts and special ornamental areas.

Mixture 3 is likely to be more hard-wearing than 1 or 2, but requires to be selected for and sown in conditions favourable to smooth-stalked meadow-grass, given adequate time and good management before use starts and managed appropriately afterwards.

(c) Medium fine turf mown at 20 mm (3/4 in) or as low as 12.5 mm (1/2 in), e.g. hockey pitches, cricket outfields, fairways, ornamental areas.

For some fairways the mixture may be modified to include perennial ryegrass, but this is unlikely to persist very well if mown at less than about 20 mm (3/4 in).

108

Mixture No.	1	2	3	4	5	6	7
Appropriate turf situation (see descriptions in text)	a,b	b,c	(b),c	c	c	d	d
			Seed percentage by weight				
Browntop bent	20	20	10	10	5	5	5
Chewings fescue	80	40	30				
Slender creeping red fescue	·	40	25	70*	40*	20*	35*
Strong creeping red fescue	·	·	·				
Smooth-stalked meadow-grass	·	·	35	·	45	40	20**
Timothy	·	·	·	20†	10†	15	·
Perennial ryegrass	·	·	·	·	·	20	40

* = blend of Chewings fescue and strong creeping red fescue, normally in equal amounts.

† = small-leaved timothy preferable.

** = on wet heavy soils good large-leaved timothy could be substituted wholly or in part.

(d)   General purpose turf mown at more than 20 mm (above ¾ in) e.g. rugger and soccer pitches.

Mixture 6 is less likely to be dominated by perennial ryegrass than Mixture 7, and may become shorter and less bulky in growth after a period of appropriate management.

Appropriate seed rates for these mixtures decrease from 35 g/m² (1 oz per sq yd) for Mixture 1 to 17 g/m² (½ oz per sq yd) (= 188 kg/ha or 1½ cwt per acre) for Mixtures 6 and 7.

Worn areas may be renovated with the appropriate mixture or, on heavily used winter pitches where damage is severe and very quick repair needed, with perennial ryegrass alone, at 17–35 g/m² (½–1 oz per sq yd). Perennial ryegrass is sometimes also used for renovating wicket ends for cricket.

(b)   Mixtures for non-intensive use

There is even less trial information from the U.K. on mixtures of this type than on those for intensive use but the Table below indicates the sort of mixtures being used. The main possible components are strong creeping red fescue and perennial ryegrass and the first decision is whether ryegrass is wanted for quick establishment. If not, Nos. 8 and 9 are broadly similar to two Dutch road verge mixtures, 9 being more suitable for very low fertility and sandy dry conditions than 8. The other two are ryegrass mixtures, 11 more dominated by ryegrass than 10. Mixtures 6 and 7 in the previous section are also often used for general situations, and many seed firms have their own prescriptions.

Mixture No.	8	9	10	11
	Seed percentage by weight			
Browntop bent	5–10	5–10	5–10	.
Fine-leaved sheep's fescue or hard fescue	.	30–40	.	.
Chewings fescue	.	10–20	.	.
Strong creeping red fescue	50–70	20–30	40–50	30–40
Smooth-stalked meadow-grass	20–40	0–15	20–30	10–20
Perennial ryegrass	.	.	10–20	50–60

II.   SEED QUALITY

The main points

There are three main aspects of seed quality which need to be considered. Two of these, analytical purity and germination, can be determined quite easily, though expensively, in laboratory tests at an Official Seed Testing Station. The third, cultivar purity, can not be assessed from inspection of seed or in a quick test, but is equally important. Grass seed for turf is now subject to

110

the new Seeds Regulations which were introduced as a result of E.E.C. entry, and various minimum standards now apply to seed sales. Details of these and of labels etc. are given in the S.T.R.I. publication 'Buying turfgrass seed in 1977'.

1.   Analytical (or species) purity

This is based on the laboratory examination of a small sample which is divided into three components (expressed as % by weight):–

(a)   Pure seed

This consists of whole normal seeds of the declared species. (If the sample is of a seeds mixture, the declared components will be listed, with the percentage of each.)

(b)   Other species

These may be reported by weight as 'weeds' and 'other crop species' or noted separately by species where special standards apply. A large number of unwanted plants may be introduced by sowing mixtures containing only a very small percentage in these two categories.

(c)   Inert matter

This includes empty seed husks and damaged seed, as well as sand, dirt, etc. Although this material has no value, some inert matter is always to be expected in most grass samples and at least it does no harm, unlike the unwanted species.

2.   Germination

This is tested by growing a sample of pure seed in a laboratory to determine the percentage that can grow in favourable conditions. Germination under relatively unfavourable field conditions may not be as high. Even new seed lots can differ greatly in germination, due to what happens at harvest and afterwards and, as seed gets older, germination progressively deteriorates. There are two disadvantages of sowing seed of low germination: not only are fewer seedlings produced but also those that do appear are liable to lack energy.

3. Cultivar purity

In general, there is no way to check that seed is true to the cultivar it should be except the lengthy one of growing the seed and examining the plants. It is, therefore, necessary to rely on certified seed, produced under supervision to ensure that seed is true to cultivar.

Seed size

In general, the larger the average seed size of a sample within the range of size for the species, the more vigorous is germination and the better the establishment of seedlings. On the other hand, less seeds are sown per unit area with a given weight of a large-seeded sample than with the same weight of a small-seeded sample. Normally, it is not necessary to worry about seed size, so long as extremes are avoided. Within any seed sample there is a range of size, and size depends more on harvest conditions, seed cleaning processes etc. than on cultivar. Nevertheless, some cultivars in a species do tend to have larger or smaller seeds than most, e.g. 'Merion' has particularly small seeds compared with most other smooth-stalked meadow-grass cultivars.

Storing seed over winter

It is sometimes necessary to keep seed from one season to the next, either as surplus to requirements or because late summer sowing was prevented. The question is often asked, 'How long can seed be stored without loss of germination?' The answer is not straightforward. Seeds are living organisms and it is almost impossible to prevent the activity of respiration even in the most ideal storage conditions of low temperature and low humidity. Thus, in any sample, some of the individual seeds are all the time ceasing to be able to produce healthy shoots. The speed of this deterioration depends on:

        (a)   the initial germination,
        (b)   the condition of the seed,
        (c)   the storage conditions.

Generally speaking the better the germination of seed when bought, the more likely it is to keep well. Good germination shows that a seed lot was harvested in good condition and hand-

112

led well afterwards. Germination that is only moderately good denotes either that the seed was damaged at some stage or that the process of deterioration has started. Once started, it generally accelerates until very low levels are reached.

Seed is best stored under dry cool conditions, kept at uniform levels without fluctuation.

Groundsmen are not likely to want to achieve very long term storage and do not normally have access to a cold store, which is the ideal, but it is not difficult to dry seed – *gently* in front of a fire or on a moderately warm radiator – and put it into a polythene bag which should be made airtight. The temperature applied to the seed should be no more than about 35°C (95°F). The bag should then be kept in a reasonably cool place, preferably where temperatures do not fluctuate too much. Obviously, if the polythene bag is opened the seed will start picking up moisture again, so it is best to leave the bag sealed until the seed is wanted.

Seed left without any special safeguard is more likely to deteriorate if left over winter in an unheated shed or outbuilding, where the relative humidity will be similar to that outdoors, than in a house or office with moderate central heating, where relative humidity is kept low and the seed is less likely to pick up moisture.

III.   TURF

1.   *Traditional mature turf*

There are three types: *(a)* specially grown turf, *(b)* inland turf from old pastures or natural grassland, or *(c)* sea-marsh turf. Most of the mature turf on the market is from old grassland and it is very variable in quality. Sea-marsh turf contains creeping bent and creeping red fescue on a silty soil.

In buying turf attention should be given to *(a)* botanical composition (including weeds), *(b)* the amount of fibre (not too little, not too much) and *(c)* the kind of soil attached – heavy soil is unsuitable for bowling greens and golf greens, sandy soil unsuitable for cricket tables. It is advisable to obtain samples for approval and to retain the approved sample for comparison with the turf delivered. There is a British Standard for turf (B.S.S. 3969) but it has reference to general landscaping purposes, not to special areas like tennis courts or bowling greens. Important factors to be decided when ordering are thickness and size. A generally suitable thickness is 30–40 mm (1¼–1½ in). If turf is too thin it handles badly, if too thick it roots less satisfactorily. Thickness should be uniform: 'boxing' is sometimes necessary to achieve this. For size, 300 mm (12 in) squares facilitate first class laying (and easy handling) but larger sizes are sometimes used – 300 × 450 mm (12 × 18 in) or 300 × 900 mm (12 × 36 in).

2. Seedling turf

Several patent turf production methods have been developed in recent years, for producing material ready to lay a few weeks after sowing. Most of these methods rely on some sort of artificial reinforcement (plastic foam or netting) to hold the young plants together. Tana grass was the first of these special turf products, consisting of densely sown grass seedlings, a few weeks old, on a thin layer of growing medium and thin polystyrene foam. It is light to carry, easy to lay in large pieces, and is grown quickly to order with the specified seed mixture. It does not, however, have much nutrient incorporated in the turf. Other products – e.g. Netlon Bravura Turf and Grass Carpet – were developed with netting incorporated in the growing medium for reinforcement. Another product, Rolawn Turf Mat, has no reinforcement but relies on root growth in a predominantly peat medium to hold the turf together; slow release nitrogen granules incorporated in the growth medium give a very vigorous turf.

All these materials, depending on the thickness and firmness of the 'turf' and the amount of incorporated nutrient, require regular watering immediately after laying and more attention to nutrition in the early months than traditional turf, and probably more top dressing and other operations to create a smooth playing surface. Suppliers' advice should be observed.

GROWTH RETARDERS

The nation spends vast sums of money each year on mowing amenity grass and it is therefore not surprising that there is a lively interest in the possible use of chemicals to restrict grass growth so as to reduce the amount of mowing and cut costs. Industry is trying to produce satisfactory materials and quite a few promising chemicals have been investigated. However, only one, maleic hydrazide has been widely available and even this seems to have had limited success in practice.

Trials by the Sports Turf Research Institute in the 1950's showed maleic hydrazide to have very limited possibilities for areas of turf normally mown very regularly, i.e. sports turf in general, because of discoloration and possible damage coupled with a non-well-groomed appearance. There seemed to be promise for use of the material on areas such as road verges etc. where standards are not so high in order to achieve a measure of economy. It is, in fact, used to some extent on such areas but not very widely.

Trials with new materials are still being made in various quarters and there are hopes of more satisfactory products becoming available. It is likely, however, that their main use will be on turf where the standards are less exacting than those on sports turf.

HEIGHT OF CUT

When grass has been mown it is impracticable to measure directly the height to which it has been cut down. Therefore 'height of cut' is usually discussed in terms of the height to which the mower has been bench set for cutting. 'Bench setting' of a roller mower involves placing a straight edge from front to back roller. The distance measured from the straight edge to the cutting edge of the bottom blade is the 'height of cut.' With a side wheel mower the straight edge passes from a side wheel to the front roller.

This method of expressing height of cut is by no means perfect and may be inappropriate for some types of machine. At best, the actual height to which the grass is cut with a given machine setting depends on the effective weight of the machine and the properties of the turf surface such as softness. Resulting variations can be of decided significance when close-mown fine turf is being considered. Nevertheless, being well understood, the method is very useful if intelligently interpreted.

HYDROSEEDING *(Hydraulic seeding)*

A recent development in turfgrass seeding techniques known as hydroseeding or hydraulic seeding involves thé use of water as a carrier for the application of seed of turfgrasses (or of other vegetation). Specialised equipment is used, including a large tank of 2250–6750 litres (500–1500 gal) in which are suitable agitators and which is fitted with a pump, hose and nozzle. After the seed has been mixed with water, the seed-in-water suspension is applied to the site by pumping it through the hose and nozzle arrangement under a pressure of about 700 kN/m² (100 lb per sq in). Fertilizer and fibre mulch may be mixed into the tank for application at the same time as the seed. In an alternative procedure the seed and fertilizer are applied in one operation which is closely followed by equipment which blows chopped straw (sprayed with an adhesive such as bitumen as it emerges) on to the site as a mulch. Hydroseeding is of particular interest for sowing grass seed on road verges, particularly where there are steep embankments and it has been widely used for this purpose in the U.S.A. It has come into use more recently in this country but there are now contractors tooled up to sow seed by the hydroseeding technique.

LAWNS

A lawn can be defined as a smooth space of ground covered with grass. It is generally understood to be near a house – a part of the garden – but lawns are also found in public places of various kinds. Lawns can vary greatly in quality, much depending on what is considered to meet requirements. It may be sufficient in some cases merely to green over an unsightly patch of earth; some lawns may be required as drying areas or as children's play areas but many proud home owners would like a high quality turf resembling that on their bowling green or golf greens. Unfortunately few of these home owners are able to provide the skill, equipment and time to achieve this.

Lay-out of New Lawns

It is not necessary to think always in terms of a square or oblong patch of lawn surrounded by borders although this is very popular indeed. Some degree of irregularity in shape and the presence of minor undulations or terracing etc. is frequently a good idea, representing some degree of landscaping. The shape and contours required should be decided in the light of all this and bearing in mind that about 150 mm (6 in) of top soil should remain overall on completion, whilst gradients should allow easy mowing in more than one direction and if possible encourage excess surface water to escape from the sides and not collect into hollows. The nature of the site and its surrounds obviously has an influence on what can be done but generally speaking simple contours or shapes with no awkward corners or mounds are most satisfactory and these can often be produced with comparatively little effort. Narrow paths between flower beds soon become 'moth eaten' and should be avoided if possible. If considerable changes in levels are required this may involve stripping the top soil before grading in the sub-soil.

Site Clearance

Any builders' debris or other rough material including tree roots which may be around should be removed and small bushes and long grass burnt.

Grading

Often a new lawn can be made without major alterations in the levels since there is no need for a lawn to be truly level, although it should, of course, be smooth to whatever gradient is achieved. A gentle slope is quite a good thing to help shed surface water during heavy rain. Minor adjustment in levels can be achieved by moving top soil, always subject to the limitation that there should be at least 150 mm (6 in), or at any rate a minimum of 100 mm (4 in) of good top soil everywhere on completion. It is often helpful to buy in a few loads of top soil to improve levels if they are such that there is difficulty in getting improvement from the surface without leaving some parts with insufficient top soil.

If considerable grading is required then unfortunately stripping the top soil so as to allow grading in the sub-soil may become necessary. Such work may for convenience have to be accomplished in sections. The top soil is heaped up in a convenient place and the sub-soil gradients altered (usually by cut and fill) before returning the top soil. To achieve satisfactory levels in this process most home owners will be able to manage satisfactorily by the use of pegs, string and possibly a straight edge but on larger sites a more sophisticated procedure may be necessary.

Care should be taken to work the soil under dry conditions if at all possible since it is adversely affected by handling in wet conditions and particularly so where relatively heavy machinery is brought in to help.

Drainage

On many sites, particularly where there has been grading, the sub-soil as well as the top soil is heavily compacted and unless this compaction is removed moisture penetration is severely impeded. On small areas double digging may be needed in order to break up both the sub-soil and the top soil but on larger areas the sub-soil cultivation is probably better achieved by means of a tractor-drawn or tractor-mounted sub-soiler which is usually best used in two directions at right-angles *after* replacement of the top soil.

The question arises as to whether any pipe drainage is required. Observations suggest that most people are able to manage without pipe drainage for their home lawns but certainly the possible need for drain pipes needs consideration since it is not possible to have a good lawn with healthy grass if the soil is waterlogged in wet weather. Sometimes a single line of clayware or plastic land tiles will suffice provided that some form of outlet can be provided. The best outlet is a connection to a main drain somewhere since soakaways, while not without merit, are not always satisfactory. On large lawns where a drainage system is required a proper herringbone system may be appropriate and whenever a drainage system is installed it is a good plan to cover the pipes with 12.5 mm (½ in) gravel blinded by course sand to within about 150 mm (6 in) of the final surface of the lawn before being finally covered with 150 mm (6 in) of top soil. There should be no sub-soil over the drains.

Digging (or ploughing for large sites) is the first operation and any old turf which exists should be buried. If this first cultivation is done in autumn or winter the soil may be allowed to 'weather' during frost. Then in the spring the land can be worked down by hand cultivators, rakes etc. (or the mechanical equivalents) in the drier spring weather. During the top soil cultivations it is wise to consider physical improvement of the soil by working in really heavy dressings of suitable lime free sand, the aim being to get an immediate surface soil with at least 75% of sand. The amount of sand to add therefore depends on how deep it is proposed to cultivate it in. On really heavy soils as much as 11 m³ per 100m² (approx 12 cu yd per 100 sq yd) can be used with advantage and the addition of some peat is also a good idea on most soils, say 3.5 kg/m² (7 lb per sq yd) of granulated peat. Light sandy land benefits from organic materials which improve moisture and plant food holding capacity. Well rotted stable manure is an excellent material but unfortunately is rather rare and usually has to be substituted by such things as leaf mould or granulated peat.

Before sowing the lawn it is wise to try and ensure that the prepared land is free from roots and seeds of undesirable plants (including weed grasses) which may establish in the new sward. A very good way of accomplishing this is to give a complete summer's fallowing, i.e. to allow the weeds to germinate and then cultivate them out repeatedly. In some cases it is convenient to grow a potato crop or other crop which gives some encouragement for the amount of work involved. Chemical herbicides are of some value but have not provided a complete answer and sterilisation is both costly and also risky for domestic lawns.

During all preparation work special attention should be given to areas expected to have heavy traffic (e.g. narrow spaces between flower beds) to try and make them fit to take the extra wear.

The turf may be established from seed or sod but the final preparations are fairly similar in that in either case we need a firm, fine soil bed and this is achieved by repeated cultivations with suitable compacting procedures. The earth may be broken up by means of a hand cultivator or its mechanical equivalent as seems more appropriate, followed by rough raking with the removal of the larger stones. To try and eliminate air pockets in

'Heeling' to firm up the seed bed and get out air pockets when preparing for a new lawn.

the body of the soil it is wise to use the old fashioned procedure of 'heeling' the surface, i.e. treading carefully with the weight of the body thrown on the heels so that soil is pressed down into the soft spots. The heel marks should be every 50 mm or 75 mm (2 or 3 in) and the operation should be carried out when the soil is dry enough not to adhere to the boots.

Further raking and heeling should follow, the final aim being to achieve a smooth surface from which small bumps and depressions have been entirely eliminated while the soil is sufficiently firm (but not over-compacted) to minimise the risk of sinkage later producing an undulating surface. In the course of the various cultivations stones bigger than about 12.5 mm (½ in) should be picked and/or raked off the site. A rather more perfect tilth is required for seeding than is required for turfing.

The possibility that the soil needs lime should be taken into account but before liming it is wise to have the soil tested in a suitable laboratory since liming is not to be undertaken lightly when a good lawn is required. If lime is required it can be applied at a suitable rate (not too high) during the various cultivations described.

Turfing

There is a widespread belief that turfing is the best way to produce a good lawn. This is not really true, although the use of turf does simplify matters for the amateur and make possible the use of less perfect soil conditions. Unfortunately really good turf is not easy to come by and is expensive and many people become disappointed with the lawns they have obtained by buying turf at a price they can afford. There is a British Standard Specification for turf for general landscaping work but the standard is not high enough for a really good lawn. There is also the point that the soil which comes with the turf may not match the existing soil and it may be ill-draining clay. The main advantage of turfing is time saving since turf can be laid in the autumn when it is too late for seeding and with good management can appear as a really good lawn the following summer. Autumn is the best time to lay turf since turf laid in spring and summer runs the risk of drying out and not establishing satisfactorily.

Turf should be bought on the basis of a sample which should show it preferably established in soil of a sandy loam nature free from stones. The turf should be of close texture with good uniform density and colour with sufficient fibre to hold the turf together for handling, although excess is a disadvantage. The quality of grasses in the turf purchased depends on the requirements but for a really good lawn there should be little in the turf except fine bent and/or fescue grasses and even for second-class lawns, weeds and disease should be absent.

The turf delivered should be in mown condition and it is best for most people in 300 mm (1ft) squares, though pieces 450 mm × 300 mm (18 in × 12 in) or 900 mm × 300 mm (3 ft × 1 ft) are also common. The turf should be of even thickness of, say, 32 mm (1¼ in) and if the turf which arrives is uneven in thickness it may be desirable to 'box' the turf, i.e. to lay the turf, roots up, in a shallow tray of suitable depth and draw a stout knife across the top edge of the box so as to bring the turf to the standard thickness.

121

Before laying the turf, the soil should receive such fertilizer treatment as is required. A soil test is helpful but usually a fairly standard mixture of a proprietary nature can be used or something on the following lines:–

	per 100 m² OR per 100 sq yd	
fine hoof and horn meal	3.0 kg	6 lb
fine bone meal	3.0 kg	6 lb
powdered superphosphate	3.0 kg	6 lb
sulphate of potash	1.5 kg	3 lb

The fertilizer should be raked in a few days before laying the turf if possible.

The soil should be reasonably dry when turfing takes place. It is usually convenient to commence by laying a single turf round the perimeter of the site; after that turfing the body of the site should be accomplished by working to face the unturfed part which should be maintained in its prepared condition. All traffic (operator and equipment) should be on planks laid across the turf and moved as required. The turf should be laid with broken joints like bricks in a wall and each turf should be laid flat and tight up to its neighbours. If any particular turf seems too high or too low adjustments should be made in the soil below rather than by beating down the turf to a level. When the whole area has been turfed it should be carefully rolled with a light roller and then a sandy compost applied at about 2.5 kg/m² (5 lb per sq yd) and carefully brushed in, some effort being made to work it particularly into the joints.

Seedling 'Turf'

New processes have recently been devised by which the supplier can produce a kind of turf from standard seeds mixtures or from any nominated seeds mixture in the time of a few weeks. The processes are, of course, of a proprietary nature and the 'turf' produced costs about the same as really good normal turf. The seedling turf is grown in a special growth medium under special conditions and is sold to a thickness of about 12.5 mm (½ in) in rolls which are quite easy to handle because they are light in weight. If this kind of 'turf' is purchased it is important to observe any special instructions or recommendations issued by the suppliers. It is also important that 'turf' of this kind should not be allowed to dry out until established and it should not be laid unless water can be applied as necessary.

Seeding

The preferred time for sowing grass seed is about the end of August. Spring sowings can be successful but they run a greater risk from drought since May is often very dry, and in the spring weed competition is usually greater than it is in the late summer. Sowing grass seed is the cheapest and probably the best way of getting a good lawn but complete satisfaction can only be achieved if sufficient skilled work is put into the whole operation and into the initial maintenance.

In the final stages of preparing the soil bed and a few days before sowing a suitable pre-seeding fertilizer should be given; this may be a reputable proprietary product but enthusiasts may care to make up their own mixture on the following lines:

	per 100 m² **OR** per 100 sq yd	
sulphate of ammonia	1.5 kg	3 lb
fine hoof and horn meal	1.5 kg	3 lb
dried blood	1.5 kg	3 lb
powdered superphosphate	3.0 kg	6 lb
fine bone meal	3.0 kg	6 lb
sulphate of potash	1.5 kg	3 lb

The fertilizer should be carefully and thoroughly raked into the soil a few days before sowing.

The kind of grass seed to use depends on the kind of lawn required (See GRASSES) and on the amount one is prepared to pay. For a first-class lawn the old fashioned mixture;-

8 parts Chewings fescue
2 parts browntop bent

is suitable, with a rate of sowing of about 35 g/m² (1 oz per sq yd). It is important to try and obtain the best cultivars of the two named grasses. For hard wearing second quality lawns or the children's playground type of lawn, coarser mixtures may be used, even including perennial ryegrass though this particular grass is decidedly coarse for lawns. There are, of course, good proprietary seeds mixtures available at various prices from reput-

123

able lawn seed suppliers who will also indicate the composition of their mixtures.

When sowing is carried out the soil bed should be in a raked condition and quite dry. It is advantageous to divide the seed into two lots for sowing in transverse directions and for really careful work on big areas it is advisable to divide the lawn into sections, weigh the quantity of seed for each section and then split this· again into two halves for transverse sowing. The seed should be carefully raked in. It is not usually necessary or desirable to roll after raking but rolling may be needed (after stone picking) when the grass is well through so as to tighten the soil round the grass roots preparatory to the first mowing and to push small stones down below the cutter blade.

Bird damage can be a problem in urban areas and some chemical preparations are sold for treating the seed – indeed most lawn seed sold may be ready treated. These treatments are of limited value unfortunately, since most of the damage done by birds tends to be the spoiling of the seed bed when the birds are having dust baths rather than the loss of seed. Once again an old fashioned approach is very good – stretching across the lawn black cotton supported a short distance from the ground by short sticks.

After Care

New lawns established from turf need occasional top dressing with bulky material such as sandy compost so as to smooth out the surface and to make sure the cracks are filled. Occasional rolling may also be required but excess is to be avoided. During its first full growing year the grass will need mowing regularly but over-close mowing should be avoided, particularly if it leads to skimming any raised pieces of turf. In the first spring following the autumn turfing a good general fertilizer might well be given as for an existing lawn.

New sown lawns should not be mown until the grass is about 50 mm (2 in) long and then the sward should be carefully topped, preferably by means of a side-wheel mower which is sharp and in good condition. Before mowing surface stones should be picked off and the area carefully rolled if necessary, the grass being allowed to regain the upright position before mowing takes place. Hand weeding of coarse grass or weeds in the new sward is to be commended, although annual weeds will disappear with mowing. The grass should not be allowed to get too long, so that regular mowing is essential with the height of cut being gradually dropped to the finally chosen height over a period of weeks. A lawn sown in the late summer or early autumn will usually need a further fertilizer treatment the following spring in the form of a general fertilizer as for an existing lawn.

Surface levels may need attention – they are unlikely to be as good as those achieved with a turfed lawn and occasional top dressing with sandy compost at, say, monthly intervals during the first full year's growth will help a great deal to produce the smooth surface which is such an attractive feature of a really good lawn.

Despite the most thorough approach to sowing a new lawn sometimes thin or bald patches show up after a few weeks and to cover this eventuality it is wise to preserve a little of the original seed so that over-sowing can be carried out immediately these patches are noticed with the result that they can catch up quickly with the rest.

Maintenance

An important characteristic of a good lawn is its uniformity in all respects. It should be uniform in texture, colour and surface smoothness without blemishes from weeds, disease, earth-worms or bad mowing. A lawn needs to be sufficiently hard wearing to stand what is required of it and should maintain a good colour throughout the year. The colour at various seasons is in part a reflection of the grass species and cultivar, in part a reflection of management including fertilization and moisture control.

Mowing

If a lawn is to be maintained in pleasing condition it is important that regular mowing is carried out but that the mowing should not be too keen. Obviously a good mower in good condition is essential but buying mowers has much in common with buying cars – personal choice as well as engineering performance and price affect the issue. For best results the most expensive conventional mower (roller type) of a suitable size may well be the best. An important feature of such a mower is the number of cuts to a linear metre (linear yard) which for really fine turf should be as much as 100 to 120, although for coarser turf a much lower number is usual. The modern home owner tends to prefer a powered mower, particularly if he has a large lawn, but it is wise to buy as light a machine as possible since regular use of a heavy machine can cause considerable soil compaction. A heavy machine, of course, is more difficult to handle from shed to lawn and on small lawns the effort of getting a powered mower on to the lawn may be greater than the effort required to push a hand mower!

Powered rotary mowers are becoming increasingly popular, possibly because of cost advantages and convenience and they are satisfactory where a really fine finish is not required. They will chop down all kinds of grass very satisfactorily and are remarkably tolerant of conditions of use but they do not usually cut very short and tend to bruise the grass so that a really fine finish is difficult to achieve.

It is a mistake to cut grass too short since no grass really thrives when it is so severely defoliated. Even if the lawn contains only the really fine grasses it should not be cut closer than, say, 6–12.5 mm (¼–½ in). For less fine lawns the height should be 12.5–25 mm (½–1 in) and for ryegrass lawns 25 mm (1 in) is more satisfactory since ryegrass does not really like cutting any shorter. The mowing should be done very regularly since this produces the best results and during the vigorous growing season a good fine lawn needs mowing as often as three times a week, whilst even a second-class lawn should be mown at least once a week. It is advantageous if a lawn can be mown in different directions each time it is cut. Less frequent mowing is necessary when growth is not very vigorous, of course, but the grass should never be allowed to get very much longer than its accepted height so that even during the winter months careful topping during mild weather conditions may be desirable. Whenever the grass is mown it is advantageous if the operation is carried out when the grass is dry. Allowing cuttings to fly results in a return of plant foods to the lawn but it is generally held to be wise to remove cuttings since they encourage disease, weeds, earthworm casting, coarse grasses and a soft surface.

Edging

Tidy edges improve the appearance even of a second rate lawn. For small lawns ordinary hand shears to cut the grass at the edges are often used but long-handled shears or special lawn edge trimmers save a lot of backache. Even when clipped regularly edges become uneven and they may therefore need attention with a spade or turf cutter, say once a year. There are decided advantages in using some kind of permanent edging of metal, wood or concrete.

Top Dressing

A smooth surface is an important characteristic of a good lawn and a smooth surface enables the grass to be mown to a uniform height without leaving longer grass in hollows and short grass or bare areas on humps. The initial preparation has a great deal to do with the smoothness of a lawn but there is usually room for improvement after this. Rolling can help considerably but unfortunately it achieves its results by causing compaction and, therefore, it is wise to keep it to a minimum. Professional groundsmen and greenkeepers achieve a really smooth surface by top dressing

A selection of lawn edge trimmers.   Edge trimming.

Small tools for the lawn owner.

the surface with bulky material of suitable texture. A good lawn owner is well advised to use a similar procedure, spreading sandy compost material over the surface by hand or shovel. The material should be spread fairly evenly and then worked into the surface by means of a drag mat or drag brush. On small areas the back of a wooden rake or some kind of lute can be used to work the material backwards and forwards until it disappears into the base of the sward and obviously during the working in processes the compost goes preferentially into hollow areas. Care must, however, be taken to avoid smothering. The rate of application of the compost depends on what the surface will absorb. An average rate might be, say, 2.0 kg/m² (4 lb per sq yd) and the most convenient time to apply may prove to be the early autumn but the lawn owner is less restricted in his choice of season than the professional turf man.

Fertilizer

Fertilizer requirements for existing lawns are very variable. Some lawns seem to go on satisfactorily for a very long time without any fertilizer at all and on rich soils the occasional dressing once every five or ten years may be all that is necessary. There is certainly a tendency for lawn owners to over-feed. On poor soils where wear on the lawn is heavy as much as two dressings of good fertilizer every year may be wanted but usually once a year is at least enough and a reputable brand of lawn fertilizer could be given each spring. Lawn owners who are keen enough to take a detailed interest in what they are doing could make up a suitable mixture as follows:-

	per 100 m² OR	per 100 sq yd
sulphate of ammonia	1.5 kg	3 lb
fine hoof and horn meal	0.5 kg	1 lb
dried blood	0.5 kg	1 lb
powdered superphosphate	2.0 kg	4 lb
fine bone meal	0.5 kg	1 lb
sulphate of potash	0.5 kg	1 lb

This fertilizer should, of course, be mixed with sandy compost or similar material to facilitate spreading and minimise scorch risk, using compost at about 14.0 kg/100 m² (28 lb per 100 sq yd). In some circumstances addition to the fertilizer mixture of 0.5 kg/100 m² (1 lb per 100 sq yd) calcined sulphate of iron is worth while to improve grass colour and check weeds and disease. Spreading of fertilizer should be done most carefully to get even distribution and it is best done during showery weather so that the material can be washed in by nature. If no rain falls within one or two days of the application watering in is usually desirable to avoid damage to the grass. An experienced professional groundsman obtains the best distribution by hand spreading and the lawn owner should not despise this method, though it needs great care. Small distributors are available but matching up the adjacent breadths to avoid missing strips or overlapping causes difficulty as does turning the ends.

Mechanical Operations

A good deal of mechanical work is important on bowling greens, golf greens etc. but usually these operations are much less important on the average lawn and often their benefit may not be worth the effort put into the job. Regular brushing or light raking helps to keep a lawn looking trim and to prevent the formation of excessive fibre at the surface. It also brings up runners of weeds like clover and, therefore, restricts their spread. If an old lawn has an excessive mat or thatch of fibre, severe scarification with a wire rake or with appropriate mechanical equipment is very useful and such work is usually best carried out at the end of the summer at a time when there is still sufficient growth to heal up any disfigurement which might be caused.

Very little rolling is necessary or desirable on a lawn. Possibly a light rolling in the spring may be needed to firm up any upheaval caused by winter frosts but often the lawn mower will do all that is wanted.

Aeration is an operation very frequently needed on sports turf areas but few lawns have the amount of use which causes over-compaction. Some kind of forking may possibly be required every three or four years with whatever equipment is most easily obtained. For the small lawn so-called hand forks are probably the best. These may have solid tines or hollow tines which remove a core of soil and thus allow the surrounding soil to expand which, of course, relieves the compaction. Forking helps to improve root development, particularly hollow tine forking, and, of course, good root development increases the resistance of grass to drought and to wear and tear. Hollow tining is the best way of relieving excess compaction but the holes in the turf can be invaded by weeds. There is little doubt that forking of any kind can be over-done but this applies more particularly to hollow tining. The average lawn does not need very much effort on aeration.

Watering

If a healthy green lawn is wanted in dry weather then some facility for watering is obviously essential. Watering is not an unmixed blessing in that it tends to encourage weed grasses and weeds but without sufficient moisture grass will not stay green and pleasant looking. Many lawn owners apply water by means of a hosepipe with some kind of rose device but a simple kind of sprinkler is regarded as much more satisfactory in getting even distribution. Watering should be started before the grass starts to wither up and if there is difficulty in getting the water to penetrate shallow spiking is often helpful.

Renovation

Even in the best regulated circles there are times when patches of lawn become bare for some reason or other and it is necessary to repair them. Sometimes it may be worth bringing a patch of turf from a less important part of the lawn to replace a patch which catches the eye. Usually, however, it is necessary to scratch up a seed bed in the earth and sow a little grass seed of a kind which will match the existing grasses. It may be necessary to protect these patches from birds. If the edges of the lawn become badly worn often the best plan is to strip the outside band of turf carefully to a width of, say, 300 mm (1 ft), to replace it with turf cut from the next 300 mm (1 ft) of the lawn and then put the worn turf in place of this. The thin turf can then be renovated with seed and soil.

Lime, weed control, moss, pests and diseases are covered in the appropriate sections.

LAWN SAND

Lawn Sand is the term applied to a mixture of sand with certain chemicals and which at one time was the nearest thing to a selective weedkiller available. A straightforward lawn sand as then used contained sulphate of ammonia and calcined sulphate of iron. There were many formulations but a common one was

> 3 parts sulphate of ammonia
> 1 part calcined sulphate of iron
> 10 parts fine sand

This was applied to weedy turf in good growth conditions at 140 g/m² (4 oz per sq yd), preferably on a damp summer morning with a fine day to follow. Under these conditions the grass was severely blackened but recovered while the majority of weeds were burned out. It was necessary to water if no rain fell within 48 hours so as to prevent the grass being too severely damaged and under the influence of the generous dressing of sulphate of ammonia, it grew vigorously.

Ordinary lawn sand as described above is now very seldom used for selective weedkilling in general, having been replaced by the new growth regulator type of herbicide. It is, however, still regarded as quite useful, especially for moss control in certain circumstances e.g. in spring on an area of fine turf invaded by moss.

Proprietary mercurised lawn sands sold for moss control consist essentially of ordinary lawn sand (not necessarily identical with the formula given above) into which has been mixed a small proportion of calomel (mercurous chloride) which is a slow acting but persistent mosskiller. (See MOSS AND ITS CONTROL).

LAWN TENNIS COURTS

The Playing Surface

For lawn tennis it is essential that the surface gives a true bounce to the ball. On grass courts the surface should be firm yet sufficiently resilient to offset fatigue and undue jarring during play. A high class grass court is still the preference of most players since its natural properties are believed to provide better playing conditions in general than non-grass courts, particularly in resilience and speed.

As with other summer sports the groundsman's year starts immediately the courts are closed and if renovations are to be successful the playing season must not be extended too long.

Autumn

In the late summer and early autumn account may be taken of observations made during the playing season as to the strengths and weaknesses of the courts and their playing surfaces. Any special problems such as wet patches or marked undulations can then be dealt with.

It is important to keep the grass growing until well into the autumn months and to this end fertilizer (See FERTILIZERS) should if possible be given shortly before play ceases, i.e. towards the end of August, but if that is not done it may be necessary to give a suitable dressing a little later. Mowing should continue as necessary, the cutters being raised to leave the grass a little longer than in the summer.

The courts should be well scarified (usually mechanically) to prevent the development of a fibrous matted surface or to eliminate excess fibre if it is already there. It is important that any severe scarification should be carried out before growth ceases so that any damage done has plenty of time to recover. Renovation of thin and bare areas should also be done; this may involve considerable seeding within the body of the courts using seed of grass (See GRASSES) which will match the existing turf to try and ensure a good cover of the fine grasses for the next season. Base lines always get worn out and whilst some clubs turf out these bare areas during the late autumn and winter, others prefer to make up levels with a soil which matches the courts (or is even a little heavier) and overseed with a grass seeds mixture which is rather more robust in the relatively young condition (which it will still be in next year) than the fine grasses within the body of the courts. All seeding should be completed as early as possible preferably before the end of September even in the South.

After a season's play the surface soil is usually decidedly compacted and some form of aeration is wanted. To avoid risk of a breaking-up surface in the following season this is normally accomplished by means of solid or slit tines rather than hollow tines. The work is usually done mechanically and a machine facilitiates repeating the operation several times over the winter. To ensure smooth levels for next season's tennis top dressing is important and this should be applied while there is still some growth. Marked depressions or mounds may have to be dealt with by temporarily lifting the turf to permit adding or removing soil below it but the minor depressions which occur all over the courts can only be corrected by top dressing. Usually medium/heavy loam soil is the most suitable material and it should have passed a 5 mm (3/16 in) screen. An average dressing might be 2.0–3.0 kg/m² (4–6 lb per sq yd), the actual amount being very much dependent on the amount the surface needs or will take. The soil should be in dry condition and applied to a dry surface in order that it can be worked into the base of the sward immediately by means of a drag brush or similar. Care must be taken to avoid leaving any turf smothered in top dressing under which it would take harm. After the initial working in of the top dressing a further drag brushing may be desirable at a later date to work in any remnants.

If the base lines or any other bare areas are turfed in the late autumn it is important to acquire suitable turf, preferably from a well maintained nursery but often taken from the surrounds or bought in from elsewhere. Obviously the ideal is to have a turf nursery so as to have just the right kind of turf when it is wanted. The turf used should be of even thickness and it should be laid on an evenly firmed prepared turf bed. A straight edge should be used to ensure that it marries in with the surrounding turf. After light rolling the turf should be top dressed, with special attention to any gaps which are apparent between turves and more top dressing used later to correct any sinkage which might occur as the turf settles. In correcting undulations and repairing base lines the use of a straight edge is really essential.

Winter

The courts should be kept under regular observation so that notice may be taken at the earliest possible stage of any disease or other damage which may occur. In mild weather it may be necessary to mow occasionally, the height of cut being a little longer than in the playing season. It may also be necessary from time to time to sweep off leaves to prevent the turf from being weakened or damaged by their presence as a wet smothering cover. Some attention to the wire netting surrounds is often needed.

Spring

When suitable ground conditions prevail in the early spring the turf should be given a thorough but not too severe rolling to settle any slight upheavals caused by the winter weather and to firm up the surface for play in the months ahead. A roller of 500–750 kg (10–15 cwt) may be necessary on some sites but great care is necessary to avoid creating excessive compaction leading to

134

drainage problems. Heavy rolling during the season should be kept to a minimum and usually where a large motor mower is used little special rolling may be necessary after the spring firm-up.

Spring scarification of a gentle kind should be carried out, especially if the turf is already too dense and fibrous and, at this time, when the weather starts to warm up overseeding of any remaining thin areas should be carried out. Under suitable conditions a balanced spring fertilizer containing all the major plant foods should be given so that the turf has started growing quite vigorously for the start of the playing season. The height of cut in the early spring should be a little higher than the summer height and as the weather improves the cutters should be lowered gradually.

Summer

In summer the main items are mowing and maintaining the markings. The usual cutting height for tennis courts during good growing weather in the summer is 6 mm (¼ in) and mowing is probably necessary two or three times a week. Regular and precise marking out is very important for the game to be played properly and to cut down on the number of disputed line decisions. Making good of worn patches as far as possible by top dressing and possibly seeding should also be a routine chore. The levels of the base lines should be maintained and this may mean, when the grass is worn off, applying heavy soil and rolling down.

It is also worth while trying to get players' co-operation to avoid over-use of preferred courts. Positive action to spread wear among the different courts is decidedly recommended and at the end of the season it is an advantage to close the courts in turn, closing the first one a little early so that the renovations can get a good start.

Occasional watering may be required in dry weather although it is appreciated that this is difficult to fit in with players' requirements. On the other hand the players would like the courts to continue to exist in good condition! Occasional fertilizer dressings (See FERTILIZERS) may be required to maintain growth and if weed control is necessary then spraying with a selective weed-killer can conveniently come at a time when there is good growth,

135

say a fortnight after a fertilizer application. The end of summer fertilizer dressing is particularly important to ensure growth in the autumn.

LICHENS

These are primitive plants occurring most commonly on walls, rocks, tree trunks etc. They occur occasionally on turf which is very weak perhaps through over-wetness, over-dryness or over-acidity. The best method of control is to ensure sufficiently vigorous grass growth by removing the cause of its weakness.

LIME

Lime is used to correct over-acidity of the soil. It has beneficial effects on soil structure but it is never applied simply for this reason.

In Agriculture and Horticulture one of three forms of lime may be used. They are burnt lime (calcium oxide), slaked lime (calcium hydroxide) and ground limestone or ground chalk (calcium carbonate). Both burnt lime and slaked lime cause considerable discoloration of the turf and so, for existing turf, ground limestone is the only form which can be applied for correcting soil acidity. Any form of lime could be used to correct acidity in seed beds but ground limestone is still the one generally favoured.

The rates to apply vary considerably depending, as they do, on the degree of acidity, the amount of correction desired and the texture of the soil. Since lime, even when necessary, encourages weeds, worms and disease it should not be applied unless soil tests prove it essential and, even then, care should be taken to avoid being over-generous.

LUTE *(or Loot)*

A piece of wood about 915 mm (3 ft) long by 75 mm (3 in) wide and 20 mm (¾ in) thick fixed to a handle so as to resemble a garden rake is the simplest form of lute. There are several variations or improvements on the basic model, the most up-to-date version being the patented Trulute which has a hinged and

A Trulute being used to work in compost.

137

reversible angle-iron frame instead of the plain piece of wood. By reciprocal movement of a lute top dressing is rubbed into the turf surface, preferentially into depressions so that smoothing out of the surface is achieved. Sizes of the Trulute are available both for hand and for tractor operation.

MACHINERY MAINTENANCE

It is important that all machinery and equipment is in a permanent state of readiness for use. Essential factors in achieving this are appropriate care and maintenance with special attention to the advice provided by the manufacturers.

Turf Cultivation Equipment

Spiking machines and scarifiers etc. should all receive thorough cleaning after use followed by attention to defects and replacements where necessary, e.g. tines should be renewed if badly worn to ensure uniform and maximum penetration. All metal parts require protection against corrosion by lubrication or painting as applicable.

Particularly with the larger equipment used on winter games areas, where there is a need for regular spiking under suitable ground conditions, there is no fixed rest period for this type of machinery. Constant attention is therefore required to ensure that spiking can be undertaken whenever the right day comes along.

Fertilizer Distributors

Routine maintenance calls for the complete emptying and cleaning of the hopper, along with thorough cleaning of all pivot points and bearings etc., immediately after use. Such work should always be followed by lubrication where necessary as recommended by the makers.

It is, moreover, good practice to carry out a further thorough cleaning before storage in order to ensure that no traces of fertilizer or chemical have been over-looked as these will rapidly cause corrosion. At the end of the growing season a check should be made of all working parts and any replacements required should be ordered and fitted as quickly as possible. Further checking and calibration should then be carried out in good time to ensure correct distribution of materials when the machine is next used.

Mowers

All mowers require thorough cleaning after use to remove grass from the gears and working parts. Where electricity is available the careful use of a wire brush attachment on an electric drill may be helpful in the cleaning operation. Thorough inspection for wear and tear should then be carried out. Before use the relationship between the cutting cylinder and the bottom blade should be checked and corrected if required. Lubrication should be carried out before or after use – or both but careless oiling before use can lead to damaging drips on the turf.

Apart from the replacement of worn parts and occasional sharpening etc. it is fairly standard practice these days to send mowers requiring major repairs to reputable service depots. This is best done as soon as possible in the winter months to avoid the many complaints which are often heard about machines not returned from service until long after spring growth has returned. These are often unjustified because despatch for repairs has been overlooked or continually put off for some obscure reason. The answer is to make sure the machines are sent off at the earliest opportunity, thus spreading demands on the service depot.

For storage purposes mowers should always be kept in a dry place, preferably off the ground and well away from fertilizers and the like. In the case of motor mowers it is wise policy to remove the sparking plug, put in a few drops of oil and turn the engine over two or three times by hand before replacing the plug. The engine should be left on the compression stroke. It is also advisable to close the throttle lever and to relieve load on cables by leaving the clutch lever in the driving position.

On all machines thorough lubrication should be undertaken and the cutting cylinder should be adjusted away from the

A selection of line marking machines.

bottom blade for the rest period, all cutting edges should be smeared with oil. Grassboxes and thrower plates must not be forgotten and after thorough cleaning a coat of paint will help their preservation.

General Storage Hints

All machinery should preferably be stored on planks or wooden floors. Unfortunately it is not always possible to store equipment ideally but at the very least it should be covered, kept dry and protected from the elements. If storage is inadequate the necessary steps should be taken to budget for suitable accommodation in order to prevent deterioration and safeguard performance.

Batteries should be removed from the units they serve and stored fully charged in warm surroundings. They require checking from time to time and should always be kept fully charged. The correct amount of electrolyte must be maintained and the top of the plates never exposed.

Pneumatic tyred wheels are best jacked up and somewhat deflated for storage. Wherever springs are involved the equipment should be blocked up to take the load from the springs and 'V' belts are best removed for storing in a cool, dry and dark place.

MARKING AND MARKING MACHINES

In sports turf management the production of a playing surface is of prime importance but final presentation of the surface to the user can be further improved or alternatively marred by marking out operations. Uniform and positive line marking is not only pleasing in appearance but is essential to participants, to referees or umpires and even to spectators for the correct interpretation of any rules involved.

Preparation of Machine and Materials

Initially the performance of any line marker depends on the cleanliness of the machine and the correct preparation of whatever material is to be used. Where solids (powders) or liquids are mixed with water the recommendations made by the manufacturers should be followed exactly. Special attention should be paid to advice regarding sieving and/or agitation. Dry marking materials must be free flowing and this calls for attention to storage prior to use.

Marking Materials

Various types of marking materials are available for machine use covering a wide range of surface conditions. Some materials are more persistent than others whilst some are better suited to hard surfaces rather than grass. An ideal marking material would be waterproof, quick drying, not easily rubbed off nor would it flake or powder.

For ordinary wet line marking slaked lime is very commonly used after mixing with water to form a thick yet free flowing fluid. Ordinary commercial whiting is also used but there is increasing popularity for commercial products similar to emulsion paints. These are very good and would perhaps be used even more if they were a little cheaper. In practice they are often extended very satisfactorily by mixing into, say, double their volume of newly prepared lime wash.

A dry line marker needs to be supplied with special commercial material consisting essentially of a fine aggregate into which is mixed a binder to achieve adhesion to the surface on contact with moisture.

It should be remembered that certain materials may gain persistency through the addition of a growth inhibitor such as maleic hydrazide whilst creosote for instance will actually kill the grass. Where temporary marking only is required such materials should, therefore, be avoided. The use of creosote and oily solvents is further restricted as they will destroy rubber compositions employed on certain absorbent wheel markers.

Turf quality in the immediate vicinity of lines can also be adversely affected by the chemical content of a marking material, e.g. products containing lime often encourage worms, weeds and fungal diseases.

Surface Preparation

The efficiency and persistency of the marking material is largely dependent on the condition of the surface upon which it is used. On grassed areas it is preferable that the clippings should be removed, at least in the vicinity of the line markings. It is also sometimes useful when marking out playing areas where a slightly longer grass cover is standard, e.g. rugby pitches, to mow shorter the grass cover along the lines that are to be marked out – this practice makes the line more conspicuous.

To facilitate precise initial marking and when re-marking broken lines it is desirable to have permanent below-ground marking pegs and it is often necessary to string out the playing area along the lines to be marked. The strings (or wires) should obviously be held taut to ensure accurate continuation of lines.

Dry Line Markers

This type of marker employs a dry marking powder containing a binder, which adheres on contact with a moist surface. The materials used are generally fairly persistent and are useful under wet, muddy conditions as well as on dry surfaces.

Dry line markers usually work on the gravity feed principle with provision for controlling the flow of material. On some models a range of line width is obtained by fitting an appropriate reducer to the line former accompanied by a compensating reduction in aperture flow.

Liquid Line Markers

There are quite a few different types of liquid line marker available, the transfer of fluid from the machine to the surface being accomplished in various ways. Briefly the most common working principles are:

(a)   Wheel to wheel transfer – fluid to the front marking wheel is transferred from a second wheel rotating in the tank.

(b)   Wheel and gravity feed – a rotating wheel transfers fluid to a chute. The fluid then flows on to an absorbent marker wheel.

(c)   Cup feed – fluid is fed to the marker wheel by a series of revolving cups which dip into the fluid.

(d)   Gravity feed – no moving parts but merely a simple gravity feed system.

(e)   Pressure pump – a vane type pump forcing marking fluid directly through a jet to the surface.

(f)   Continuous belt – a continuous rubber belt which revolves in the tank is in constant contact with the ground.

In addition to the 'simple' single line marking machine there are models with off-set marking wheels and with various types of boom attachments for simultaneous 'lane marking' on running tracks etc. In certain circumstances or for the odd 'touching up' the old method of brush marking may be preferred or called for.

Using the Line Marker

The machine should always be kept in a clean condition so that flow properties are in no way impeded. Any compensating adjustments should be carried out when the need arises and parts subject to wear such as bearings should be renewed when necessary. Where an absorbent band is used on the marking wheel, the band needs renewing regularly to maintain performance. Flow mechanisms and control must always be in first class working order. For optimum performance from liquid line markers correctly prepared marking fluid (sieved if necessary) is essential.

A good playing area which has been carefully looked after for months or even years deserves the best possible line marking; careless and inferior line marking distracts from previous efforts. The enthusiasm of the operator is not always enough; the line markers as well as the materials he uses must be in tip-top condition and then used correctly to obtain the desired results.

MARL

Marl is a calcareous clay which gained a high reputation for producing good cricket wickets particularly at County level. Typically the material comes from the Nottingham area ('Nottingham marl') and is available in two grades – medium and fine. It is commonly recommended that marl put on in the autumn should be medium grade while if it is applied in the spring the fine grade should be used. Used as a top dressing the marl smooths out the surface and, because of its clay nature it rolls out (under the right moisture conditions) to produce a flat, solid surface which holds together very well.

The groundsman keys the marl into the existing surface as much as possible by spiking before and after application. Nevertheless marl used alone produces definite layers in the profile which can be disadvantageous. It is, therefore, used more commonly these days in admixture with top soil to improve adhesive and other qualities of the soil which might not otherwise be adequate and the proportions might be 20–30% marl with 80–70% soil.

METRICATION IN SPORTS TURF· CONSTRUCTION AND MANAGEMENT

The United Kingdom is gradually changing over to the metric system and the Metrication Board prepared a co-ordinated programme for metrication in agriculture, horticulture and associated industries. The programme included a series of planned targets for the individual industries and boards involved so that by the end of 1976 the changeover was to be practically complete.

A list of symbols, abbreviations and approximate conversions is given below. These are intended more as a guide than as a 'ready reckoner.' As was the case with decimal conversion of the coinage, it is essential to learn to *think* as soon as possible in terms of the new system instead of constantly converting back to the old. Manufacturers' instructions should be followed exactly when fertilizers, fungicides, selective weedkillers etc. are being used. For such work it is unwise to carry out rough conversions from imperial to metric measures and vice versa.

METRIC EQUIVALENTS

Imperial to Metric

Metric to Imperial

Length

1 in	= 25.4 mm (millimetres)	1 mm (millimetre)	= 0.039 in (inch)
1 ft	= 304.8 mm	1 cm	= 0.394 in
1 yd (yard)	= 914.4 mm	1 m (metre)	= 3.281 ft (feet)
1 mile	= 1.609 km (kilometre)	100 m	= 109.361 yd
		1 km	= 0.621 mile

Mass

1 oz (ounce)	= 28.350 g (grammes)	1 g	= 0.035 oz
1 lb (pound)	= 0.454 kg (kilogramme)	1 kg	= 2.205 lb
1 cwt (hundredweight)	= 50.802 kg	50 kg	= 110.231 lb
		1 t (tonne)	= 0.984 ton
1 ton	= 1.016 t (tonnes)		

Area

1 sq in	= 645.2 mm² (6.452 cm²)	1 mm²	= 0.00155 sq in
		1 cm²	= 0.155 sq in
1 sq ft	= 0.093 m²	1 m²	= 10.764 sq ft
1 sq yd	= 0.836 m²	1 m²	= 1.196 sq yd
1 acre	= 0.405 ha (hectare)	1 are (100 m²)	= 119.598 sq yd
		1 ha	= 2.471 acres
1 sq mile	= 259 ha = 2.59 km²	1 km²	= 0.386 sq miles

145

Volume

1 cu in	= 16.387 cm³	1 cm³	
1 cu ft	= 0.028 m³	= 1 ml	
1 cu yd	= 0.765 m³	[millilitre]	= 0.061 cu in
1 pt (pint)	= 0.568 litre	1 m³	= 35.315 cu ft
1 gal (gallon)	= 4.546 litre	1 m³	= 1.308 cu yd
		1 litre	= 1.760 pt

Weight of Water

1 gal weighs 10 lb

1 litre weighs 1 kg

Pressure

The unit is the Newton per square metre (N/m²), sometimes called a pascal (Pa)

1 lb per sq in	= 7 kN/m²
	(6.90 kN/m²)
20 lb per sq in	= 138 kN/m²

Temperature

Celsius (= Centigrade) °C

To convert A°F (Farenheit) to B °C (Celsius) use the formula
$(A-32) \times 5/9 = B°C$

Freezing point of water   32°F = 0°C

Boiling point of water   212°F = 100°C

Fahrenheit °F

To convert L °C to M °F use the formula
$(L \times 9/5) + 32 = M°F$

Commonly accepted minimum temperature for plant growth 42°F = 5.5°C.

USEFUL APPROXIMATIONS FOR SPORTS TURF

Fertilizer, Top Dressing, Seed Rates etc.

1 oz per sq yd	= 35 g/m²	(33.90 g/m²)
1 lb per sq yd	= 0.5 kg/m²	(0.54 kg/m²)
1 lb per 100 sq yd	= 0.5 kg/100 m²	(0.54 kg/100 m²)
1 lb per 1000 sq ft	= 50 kg/ha	(48.82 kg/ha)
1 cwt per acre	= 125 kg/ha	(125.53 kg/ha)
1 ton per acre	= 2.5 t/ha	(2.51 t/ha)

Watering

1 gal per sq yd	= 5 litre/m²	(5.44 litre/m²)
1 in rainfall	= 22,600 gal per acre	
25 mm rainfall	= 250,000 litre/ha	

Spraying – (weedkillers, fungicides, insecticides etc.)

1 lb per acre	= 1 kg/ha	(1.12 kg/ha)
1 gal per acre	= 10 litre/ha	(11.23 litres/ha)
1 oz in 6 gal water per 40 sq yd	=35 g in 30 litres water/40 m²	
	(33.91 g in 32.62 litres/40 m²)	
1 pt in 20 gal water per acre	=1.5 litre in 200 litres water/ha	
	(1.404 litres in 225 litre/ha)	

Drains

'2 ft to invert'	= '600 mm to invert'	(609.60 mm)
'6 in drainage carpet'	= '150 mm drainage carpet'	(152.40 mm)

Depth of Growing Medium

'10 in firmed depth of soil/sand/peat mix'	= '250 mm firmed depth of soil/sand/peat mix'	(254.00 mm)

Height of Cut

'mown at 3/16 in'	= 'mown at 5 mm'	(4.76 mm)
'mown at 1 in'	= 'mown at 25 mm'	(25.40 mm)
'mown at 2 in'	= 'mown at 50 mm'	(50.80 mm)

Reference

Going Metric: Farming and Horticulture. (1975). Metrication Board.

MOSS AND ITS CONTROL IN TURF

Introduction

The term 'moss' covers many different species, as there are over six hundred different mosses in Britain, a fact which is often overlooked by many people to whom they are all simply 'moss'.

This is perhaps because most mosses are small and many are not easily distinguished without careful examination. Fortunately, only a few species are at all common in turf and it is not too difficult to learn to recognise them.

Life History

The moss plant does not produce seeds and instead, distributes itself by varous other means, one of which is by producing very small spores in a stucture called a capsule. This is often easily seen at various times of the year. The spores are dispersed by the wind and when they germinate they produce a thread-like structure called the protonema. This can sometimes be seen on the surface of the ground, where it looks rather like a green alga. At this stage the moss plant is very susceptible to drought as the protonema is a very delicate structure not adapted to withstand dry conditions. This tends to restrict mosses to areas where at least at some time there is a plentiful supply of surface moisture. On the protonema a bud forms which gives rise to the form of the moss plant most familiar to the greenkeeper or groundsman. Moss can spread not only by spore production, but also by detachment of fragments of the plant which can establish to produce new plants.

Types of Moss

The mosses found in turf can be divided roughly into three types. These are: 'trailing,' 'upright' and 'cushion'.

The 'trailing' types are usually delicate mosses with a form of branching which gives the plant a fern-like appearance. The stems often trail over the soil surface and this mode of growth can lead to the formation of quite extensive patches. Examples of such mosses are *Hypnum cupressiforme* and *Eurhynchium praelongum*. The 'upright' types are usually fairly tall and have stiff, dark green leaves. Often only the topmost leaves on a stem are green, lower ones being brown. An example of this type of moss is *Polytrichum juniperinum*. The 'cushion' types are those in which all the small, upright unbranched stems are very close together and thus form a cushion. This is usually soft to the touch and often a dark green colour. An example of this type is *Bryum* sp.

1. *Low Fertility.* Moss often invades turf where fertility levels are too low for satisfactory grass growth. A healthy grass sward makes it difficult for the moss to establish as there is intense competition. However, if the grass is weak due to lack of adequate nutrition, the balance of competition is altered and the moss, which is less demanding so far as fertility is concerned, gets a better chance. Similarly, soils which are too acid will tend to be invaded by moss. The acidity can be corrected by liming but this should *not* be done unless analysis of soil samples has demonstrated the need for liming.

2. *Moisture.* The 'upright' type of moss, e.g. *Polytrichum,* is often found in dry conditions, commonly occurring on ridges and banks where the soil is dry and grass growth not so vigorous. However, most mosses found in turf are encouraged by moist conditions; their thin leaves and the delicate protonema are easily damaged by drying out. The dependence on moisture accounts for the fact that moss, particularly the 'trailing' type is commonest in wet years and less obvious in the summer than the winter. However, surface moisture can be permanently sufficient to allow moss growth and this may be due to poor drainage of the whole soil or compaction of the surface layers.

3. *Mowing.* Mowing has a marked influence on moss growth. Fine turf areas that are cut too closely, e.g. repeated mowing at 3 mm (⅛ in) or less are often invaded by the 'cushion' type of moss. Even where the correct height of cut is being used, if levels are not sufficiently true there may be scalping of some parts. The reason for the moss invasion is the thinning of the grass cover because no grass species flourishes under repeated mowing at a height of cut of less than 5 mm (3/16 in).

The opposite condition, i.e. leaving the grass too long, tends to encourage the 'trailing' type of moss because turf with long grass will often have more surface moisture and will frequently be a less dense sward.

4. *Light.* Moss is often seen in shady places, e.g. under trees. This is partly due to the lower light levels weakening the grass

and lessening the competition but the increased moisture, characteristic of such situations, is another factor.

Combinations of factors

So far the factors encouraging moss have been considered individually. In practice it is unusual for a single factor to be to blame. Instead it is usually a combination of several, none of which by itself is sufficiently bad to cause the trouble. An example of such a situation would be an area, possibly not receiving quite enough fertilizer, subjected to fairly dry conditions in the summer (when, therefore, the sward was weakened) and inadequately drained in winter. Then moss invasion may accompany the coming of moist conditions in autumn.

Moss Control

1. *Management.* From the above it should be realised that moss is often an indicator of faulty growing conditions. Steps should be taken to correct these conditions as far as possible to discourage the moss and favour growth of grass. It is often possible to eliminate moss by changes in management, e.g. attention to surface levels, correct mowing practices, improved aeration and better drainage where necessary. However, sometimes circumstances may prevent moss removal by this means. An example of this is where important trees are causing moisture and low light problems which can not easily be alleviated. In these cases some assistance can be obtained by chemical means. Mosskillers can also be applied as a short-term measure to suppress the growth of moss whilst correction of the predisposing factors is being undertaken. Long term control is seldom achieved by chemical mosskillers alone.

2. *Chemicals used in Moss control.* The most commonly used compounds are calomel (mercurous chloride), a slow-acting but long-lasting treatment, and calcined sulphate of iron, which has a burning-out effect but is not persistent.

An old-established mosskiller for spring and summer use is 'lawn sand'. This combines sulphate of ammonia, calcined sulphate of iron and sand, which is the carrier to give sufficient bulk

150

How mercurised lawn sands can control moss, the left hand side having been treated some weeks before the photograph was taken.

for application. The proportion of the materials varies in different commercial products but 3:1:10 is a mixture which has given successful results. This might be given at a rate of 136 g/m² (4 oz per sq yd). With lawn sand, some temporary darkening of the grass is to be expected but it is encouraged by the fertilizer to fill in the space left by the moss.

Calomel used alone prevents spore germination and is very slow to act, in some cases not having any noticeable effect for twelve months after treatment. However, it is used advantageously in admixture with sulphate of ammonia and sulphate of iron plus carrier to produce proprietary mercurised lawn sands for spring and summer use or in admixture with sulphate of iron plus carrier and with little or no nitrogen for autumn and winter use. The commercially available products often, because of cost, do not contain as much calomel as to ensure effective control and it is a matter for regret that some firms do not say how much is, in fact, present. Nevertheless it is definitely not advisable to mix

151

one's own mercurised lawn sand or mercurised mosskiller because of the toxicity risk. The maker's recommended rate of application for commercial calomel mosskiller is usually about 136 g/m² (4 oz per sq yd).

Other materials are used as mosskillers and some of these are available commercially. Dichlorophen and chloroxuron are two substances which are relatively recent additions to the range of mosskillers and these materials seem to be effective. However, proprietary products containing them may be fairly expensive.

The cost of mosskilling can be high, especially if large areas are to be treated. Even ordinary lawn sand is expensive, while the cost in time and labour to apply the materials must also be considered. This makes attention to correct management practices even more desirable.

MOWING AND MOWING MACHINES

Mowing is generally the most time consuming and costly item involved in amenity turf maintenance. How it is done and how often, materially affect the turf in various respects – sward composition, density and vigour, weediness, worm activity, disease occurrence, fibre build up, etc.

The kind of turf involved and the requirements from it influence the approach to mowing. There is a wide variation from the fine turf of bowling greens and putting greens which require mowing very keenly and frequently, through general sports areas which require mowing much less keenly and perhaps only once a week, to road verges and parkland which may only need mowing a very few times a year to keep tidy – if they are mown at all!

Choice of Machinery

A range of machinery is available to suit all situations and obviously the machine used should have been chosen to fit the situation.

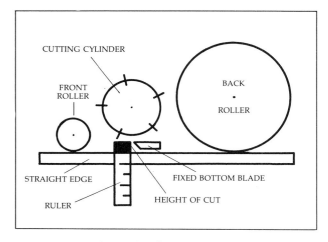

CUTTING CYLINDER

FRONT
ROLLER

BACK

ROLLER

STRAIGHT EDGE

FIXED BOTTOM BLADE

RULER

HEIGHT OF CUT

Setting a mower for height of cut.

A motor mower for use on a tennis court or cricket table.

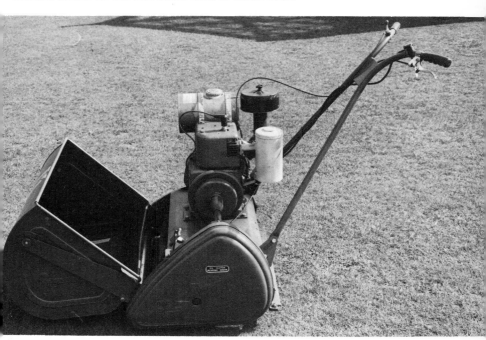

On small lawns hand mowers are most widely used but powered conventional mowers (petrol or electric driven) are now more common particularly on larger lawns and many people nowadays use powered rotary mowers for economy and convenience. On most sports turf areas power driven conventional cylinder type mowers are preferred for producing a good finish and in general the greater the number of cuts per metre run (which is related to the number of blades on the cylinder and its speed of rotation), the finer the finish. For a really fine finish as on a bowling green, we need at least one hundred cuts per metre run. Individual winter pitches or small cricket grounds are often mown with large motor mowers but for bigger grounds, racecourses, golf fairways, etc. gang mowers are widely used.

On golf courses the last couple of years have seen the introduction of the so-called triple mowers which, though representing expensive and sophisticated machinery, are proving popular for mowing golf greens because of their speed of operation and because they can be fitted to carry out other operations such as scarification.

For the miscellaneous areas that require keeping tidy – golf roughs, road verges, etc. – a variety of handy mechanical equipment is brought into use – various rotary mowers, flail machines and even reciprocating mowers based on the same principle as the machines farmers have long used for cutting hay.

By and large it can be safely assumed that for any area an appropriate machine can be found.

Maintenance of Equipment

The obvious requirement that for good mowing one needs a good mower in good working order is not always observed. Maintenance should be kept to a high standard and defects made good at the earliest opportunity. Adequate housing is another important requirement.

For most people autumn and winter provide a good opportunity to organise a thorough overhaul of mowing equipment and it is recommended that this be done as early as possible to 'get it in the queue' with repair people if necessary. The position should not be allowed to arise that grass growth has started in the spring and working mowers are not available!

154

Frequency of Mowing

In this country it has always been assumed that all amenity turf must be mown regularly but there is now a vociferous conservationist lobby for reducing or eliminating mowing on such areas as road verges. There are however some verge situations where occasional mowing is necessary for safety reasons.

National expenditure on mowing of road verges, parks, housing estate lawns, cemeteries etc. is tremendous and those responsible for management have to strike a compromise between what they might like to do and what can be afforded.

As regards sports turf, the general principle is that the more frequently the operation is carried out the better the turf, particularly in the case of very fine turf. Infrequent cutting, when it means allowing the grass to grow relatively long and then cutting it down short, weakens the turf thus leading to thinness and invasion by weeds, including moss. During the main growing season general sports grounds usually require mowing once a week and fine turf for bowling greens and golf greens as often as three times a week or more. At no time should excessive amounts of growth be allowed to remain uncut and even in the winter months occasional topping in mild weather is sometimes necessary – though not often on winter playing pitches where wear and tear keep the grass down remarkably well!

Height of Cut

The height at which grass should be cut depends on the use of the area concerned and on the grass species contained – the two are probably related.

For fine turf, users like the grass cut as close as possible but even with the fine fescues and bents the turf will not stand regular cutting closer than 5 mm (3/16 in). For this height a very true surface is required or scalping will weaken the turf and allow invasion by weeds. To ensure fast bowling and putting surfaces it is wise to cut more frequently rather than more closely. Cricket is, of course, a special case and wickets are mown down very severely indeed for a given match at, say, County standard but this state of affairs is usually only for a short period. High class tennis courts with a fine sward may be mown at 5 mm to 6 mm (3/16 in to ¼ in) but for many people 12.5 mm (½ in) is close

Gang mowers in action.

A motor mower for cricket outfields etc.

A small rotary mower which might be used for lawns.

enough. At the beginning and end of the year the height of cut on fine turf areas can usefully be increased a little to 8 mm (5/16 in) and it is important not to mow too keenly too early in the year since if close mowing is followed by cold weather the grass may receive a severe set-back.

General purpose sports areas frequently contain ryegrass and this will not easily stand regular mowing at a height less than about 25 mm (1 in). This is satisfactory for most soccer users and the rugger people like a little more grass, say 50 mm (2 in). Horse racing likes more grass still and 75 mm (3 in) seems to be the acceptable height.

On many established turf areas it is advantageous to raise the height of cut a little during dry weather if watering is not possible.

Removal of Clippings

Allowing clippings to fly keeps up fertility through the re-cycling of plant foods etc. but there are disadvantages with this approach in that, for example, the cuttings may contain weed seeds which spread weeds throughout the turf while the cuttings, in decomposing, provide first-class worm feed and so encourage earthworm activity and the production of casts while turf receiving cuttings tends to be softer and to wear more easily. For fine turf areas there is little doubt that boxing off the clippings is well worth while. Even on the large area of sports fields there is much to be said for removing the clippings. Where only an odd pitch is concerned many people use a large motor mower with grassbox and so collect their cuttings but on general sports grounds economy necessitates the use of gang mowers which do not collect cuttings and, of course, if there were machines which would collect cuttings on such large areas there would be a severe practical problem in handling the volume of grass cuttings. When, through some slip, grass on these large sports areas has got very long it is important not to allow clumps of cuttings to lie on the surface and weaken the underlying grass as well as encourage disease. With regular mowing the problem should not arise but, if it does, it may be necessary to rake off.

Weather Conditions

All practical men know that the best results from mowing are produced when the grass is dry. Where there are 'resident' staff this can in the main be achieved but where travelling staff are involved, as in most school playing field schemes and in contract

158

Medium-large rotary mower.

work, mowing unfortunately has to take place when the men and equipment arrive, more or less regardless of the conditions.

Some Common Mowing Faults

Skinning or scalping of the turf occurs where the height of cut is set too low, particularly on uneven ground.

Ribbing of the turf is usually caused either by allowing the grass to grow too long before cutting or by not having the machine properly adjusted.

Uneven cutting can arise from various practical things, e.g. if there is a different height at the two sides of the machine the adjustment may be wrong or the bottom blade may be bent or broken.

'Chewing' of the grass instead of producing a clean cut suggests that the mower blades are either very blunt or not set correctly.

159

Here are shown two examples of modern triple mowers for fine turf such as golf greens.

Washboarding – the production of pronounced wave-like ridges 150–300 mm (6–12 in) apart at right angles to the direction of mowing – is commonly associated with regular mowing in one direction and even on the same lines. The effect may be in the soil as well as in the grass. It is a good plan on all turf areas which are regularly mown to change the direction of mowing regularly to avoid washboarding and to ensure a satisfactory finish.

Safety

All powered machinery is potentially dangerous – and this includes mowing equipment! Groundsmen and greenkeepers have occasionally suffered amputations of fingers and toes through a moment's inattention or carelessness. Care must be taken when making any adjustment to engine or cutters, that the machine is safely switched off. The sparking plug should be removed before doing anything to the cutters of rotary mowers.

PATCHING WORN AREAS

Bare patches can be repaired by means of seed or turf as mentioned in the sections dealing with different kinds of turf area.

If seed is to be sown a seed bed should be prepared by the most appropriate means. This may sometimes mean forking up but in any case raking is usually necessary. Grass seed is sown to produce a sward matching existing turf and carefully raked in.

The procedure for patching with turf depends on the size of the bare patch. There are available cutters generally similar to the hole cutters used on golf greens but varying in size up to 250 mm (10 in) in diameter; there are rectangular ones as well as round ones. Within their size limits these can be used to take out the bare piece and to replace it with turf of the exact size. In the absence of one of these a good fit for patches of up to 300 mm (1 ft) or so in diameter can be ensured by placing a suitable rectangular piece of replacement turf over the irregular shaped bare patch and then, by means of a half moon, cutting the old turf round the edges of the new turf. This enables a piece to be taken out into which the patch will just fit. Care needs to be taken to ensure correct levels and the final operation is the rubbing in of a small quantity of suitable top dressing.

When repaired by seed or turf the patches should not be allowed to dry out.

PEAT

The use of sand to ameliorate top soil in the production of freely-draining root zones or top dressing materials produces mixtures which have poorer retention of moisture and nutrients than the original soil. Very sandy natural soils may also have a poor moisture holding capacity. To remedy this, organic materials are added and peat is a very popular material. Peat increases the moisture holding capacity of sandy soil and helps to regulate the supply of some nutrients to the plants. New turf will have more resilience with peat incorporated into the root zone.

The peat used should not contain a high proportion of mineral matter as this will be left as a fine residue to block the soil pores after the organic portion of the peat has decomposed. A high proportion of fine organic material is also undesirable. A relatively undecomposed fibrous peat will tend to keep the soil open and allow easy root penetration in the important early months of establishment.

Peat used in top dressing material for fine turf should be fairly finely ground (as opposed to finely divided and greasy through decomposition). Coarser granulated peat may be used on coarser turf.

NOTE   Whilst peat is undoubtedly the most important of the organic materials used by the sports turf industry, other sources of organic matter are used – such as sawdust, shredded bark, the organic residues of crops, sewage waste, composted grass clippings and not forgetting well rotted farmyard manure when obtainable.

162

PESTS AND PEST CONTROL

In comparison to many other parts of the world where a wide variety of insects and other pests causes serious damage to turf, the British Isles are relatively free of animal species likely to cause problems for the groundsman or greenkeeper. There are, however, a few species which can be troublesome and which may require specific control treatment, the chief of these being the ubiquitous earthworm.

Earthworms

Of the 25 indigenous species of earthworm, only two are responsible for trouble on turf areas. Known scientifically as *Allolobophora longa* and *A. nocturna,* these two worms are the only two which produce surface casts. Casts are unsightly, may interfere with play, cause muddy conditions, provide ideal seedbeds for weed germination, bring to the surface buried weed seed and may smother a small area of fine turf. Worm burrows may form useful drainage channels but the fine material of casts often seals the surface and interferes with surface water penetration. The casting habit apart, worms are beneficial in aerating the soil and in breaking down organic matter but wormcasts in large numbers are a nuisance and the earthworm is therefore usually eliminated, at any rate in fine turf.

Two approaches to worm control are possible – cultural control and chemical control. Both methods of reducing worm activity are used on intensively managed turf areas but chemical control, because of cost, is rarely used on extensive areas of turf.

Cultural Control

Worms are encouraged by certain soil factors and discouraged by others so it is possible to reduce the likelihood of serious worm infestation of a fine turf area by modifying the state of the soil. The casting species do not survive in soils which are very acid – pH 5.0 is about their limit. It is therefore possible to have a soil which is so acid that earthworm activity practically ceases

163

although unfortunately grass growth is likely to suffer at very low pH's too. One can, however, strike a balance, having a slightly acid soil which favours fine grass growth and which discourages, but does not entirely eliminate, the earthworm. Mowing practices also affect the worm population – allowing clippings to fly provides the worm with a ready supply of food material and boxing off should therefore be a rule on fine turf. The use of organic fertilizer materials should also be limited for the same reason.

Soil conditions are made less acidic, and therefore more suitable for earthworm activity, by the use of alkaline materials such as sea sand or alkaline fertilizers like nitrate of soda etc. The application of lime to correct over-acidity should be carried out on sports turf only when necessary to correct over-acid conditions shown by soil test.

It is possible to minimize the risk of serious worm invasion on fine turf by careful management but, even on the best managed fine turf areas, more drastic methods of worm control are often needed. On coarse turf less acid conditions are necessary for the growth of grasses such as ryegrass and cultural control of worms is more difficult. Further, on the extensive areas of football fields and the like the cost of chemical control of worms is often prohibitive.

Chemical Control

Traditionally, chemical control of worms was carried out by using one of a number of expellent wormkillers, i.e. materials which bring the worms to the surface without necessarily killing them, the worms then being swept off. Chemicals which have been widely used in the past include derris dust, mowrah meal, potassium permanganate, copper sulphate and mercuric chloride. In the main these chemicals have been superseded by poisons which actually kill the worm beneath the surface and which may give effective control for a far longer period of time.

It is unfortunate that there are, as yet, no selective wormkillers, i.e. materials which will kill casting species without harming the others.

An old-established worm poison, now less frequently used, is lead arsenate, a highly effective wormkiller which is used at

50–70 g/m² of the powder (1½–2 oz. per sq yd). Lead arsenate usually gives control for a period of several years and therefore, more often than not, justifies its somewhat high cost. Occasionally, inexplicable failures occur when lead arsenate is used and, if wide-scale use is contemplated, it is wise to test the material on a small area beforehand to ensure its effectiveness under local conditions. Lead arsenate is toxic to humans (it is now available only to professional users) and must be handled with due respect.

A more widely used worm poison these days, is chlordane, used either as a 20% granular material applied at 67–90 kg/ha (60–80 lb per acre or about 1/5 oz per sq yd) or as a 25% liquid, used at 56 litre/ha (5 gal per acre) suitably diluted, the latter being rather more efficient. Chlordane can usually be relied upon to give one year's control and cases of three years' effective control are by no means uncommon. Chlordane works out cheaper than lead arsenate. Like lead arsenate it is a highly toxic material and every precaution should be taken in its use.

A far safer material to handle is carbaryl (sevin) which, when used at 6.7 kg of the 50% material per hectare (6 lb per acre), controls worms effectively but usually for a short period of months only. Like chlordane or lead arsenate, it kills the worms beneath the surface but differs in being less toxic to humans or animals and it is believed to cause less residual damage to soil organisms.

Worm control measures are usually best taken in the autumn (or possibly spring) during mild, moist weather when the worms are actively working in the top few inches of soil and therefore more likely to contact the wormkilling agent. Preliminary spiking is sometimes desirable to aid chemical penetration into the soil and watering in, even of the dry materials, is recommended in order to wash toxic materials off the surface so that they are less likely to harm players, domestic animals or birds.

Insect Pests

Insect pests of turf are fortunately few. However, quite substantial damage to turf is occasionally caused by larvae of the daddy-long-legs or crane-fly, particularly on seaside golf courses. The grubs, commonly called leatherjackets, are hatched in the soil in the autumn and feed on the roots and basal shoots of the grass plant until the following spring when the damage usually becomes most obvious in dry weather. If leatherjackets are present in large numbers (infestation of 1200 per m² [1000 per sq yd] has been recorded) then, as a minimum, yellowed patches of turf result and the turf may, in fact, be killed off in large patches.

Control can be effected by using Gamma HCH insecticide, using a 3½% powder at the rate of 35 g/m² (1 oz per sq yd). Lead arsenate at 17 g/m² (½ oz per sq yd) or chlordane at 18.75 litre/ha (15 pints per acre) of the 25% liquid suitably diluted are also effective. Obviously, to be worth while the treatments must be applied before the damage is done to the roots of the grass. This usually means the autumn. By the time the damage is seen in the spring the grubs are likely to be pupating so that it is not much good applying treatment.

In some districts, particularly on light land which is well wooded, epidemics of garden chafer grubs occur occasionally though rarely. Extensive damage is done as a result of the grubs devouring the roots of the grass and much secondary damage is caused by birds searching for grubs. Methods of control in turf have not been fully investigated. The large cockchafer is only rarely found in British turf but it is sometimes a serious pest on the Continent. On the Continent also severe damage has occasionally been reported from 'cutworms', the larvae of certain night flying moths. Mole crickets are only occasionally found in Britain but they are sometimes a serious pest on the Continent, e.g. in Spain.

Various fly larvae occur in turf as they do in most grassland. *Dilophus* (fever fly) and *Bibio* spp. are the most often reported. The larvae are smaller than leather-jackets, being at most only about 12 mm (½ in) long and, unlike leather-jackets they have a distinct dark shiny head. They do far less damage than do leather-jackets and are rarely present in sufficient numbers to justify control measures. However, when such measures are needed the larvae can be treated in the same manner as leather jackets, although it may only be necessary to treat part of the affected area as they usually occur in clusters or nests.

Aphids (small sap-sucking insects such as green fly, black fly etc.) are sometimes seen in large numbers on the leaves of long

166

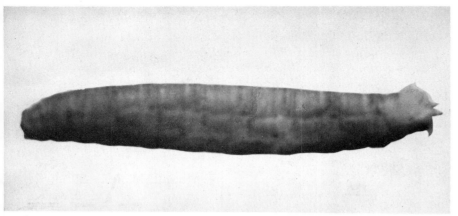

The grub of the cranefly – the leather jacket (magnified 5 times).

grass. They may cause considerable damage especially in dry conditions and seem to be a more serious problem following a mild winter. They are less commonly seen on closely cut grass but may occur very occasionally. They are often untreated as the cost of the damage is thought to be insufficient to justify the cost of treatment. However, a heavy infestation of a fine turf area may be treated with a systemic insecticide, for example dimethoate.

Eelworms

Eelworms (nematodes) have been found occasionally in sick or dead grass plants. They are microscopic creatures (0.5 mm – 1.5 mm) in length, sharp pointed at one or both ends, and transparent so that their internal organs are visible. Nematodes are extremely common in soil and water and may be found associated with healthy plants.

Some eelworms, however, are the cause of important plant diseases (e.g. in potatoes and tomatoes) and recently there have been reports of turf diseases which might be caused by eelworms. These reports have mostly been from the U.S.A. but there have been one or two cases in this country where it has seemed that the cause of turf taking on a yellow unhealthy appearance has been eelworms.

167

Moles often cause serious turf damage and can be controlled by trapping, gassing with exhaust fumes or smoke bombs, or by poisoning with earthworms dipped in the deadly poison strychnine. Written authority (available for professional users only) must be obtained from the Divisional Office of the Ministry of Agriculture before this substance can be used. One of the best methods of mole control is an indirect one – moles feed almost entirely on earthworms, so a worm-free area is far less prone to mole trouble.

Rabbits are often troublesome, particularly on newly sown or newly renovated areas. They can be trapped or shot until reduced by the appearance of a new myxomatosis strain. Small seeded areas can be protected by wire netting covers or similar. In general, commercial rabbit repellents have not been found very effective.

Birds, particularly crows and seagulls, are often annoying as they pick up divots or repaired holes on golf courses and other sports turf areas while looking for insects. Damage can often be minimized by eliminating the insect which the bird is looking for. In some cases birds attack fibrous turf areas in a search for nesting material; obviously such excess fibre should be eliminated by effective management including scarification work. Direct action against birds should be undertaken only after due reference to Bird Protection regulations!

RACECOURSES

The kind of surface and the kind of maintenance required for racetracks are not very different from those wanted for winter pitches. The tracks are required to stand very hard wear and this results in a need for a good deal of restoration. Uniform going of the right quality is all-important and the sites for the older racecourses such as Ascot and Newmarket were probably chosen deliberately because of the naturally springy turf since this kind of turf found on heaths and downs is so highly regarded for both training and racing. Such turf with careful maintenance will stand a great deal of wear but, unfortunately, once over-use has resulted in a complete break-down of the matted turf it is impossible to re-establish it in an acceptable period of time. Many modern racecourses therefore rely for cushioning on extra length of grass. 75 mm (3 in) is common although some people seem to think they need as much as 150 mm (6 in)!

Soil moisture control is very important on racecourses and probably deserving of more attention than it receives. The cancellation of race meetings in wet weather suggests that drainage of the tracks is not all that it should be, at any rate on some of the courses used in winter, and no doubt the cost of draining such large areas has much to do with this. Cost (and supply) considerations may also affect the approach to efficient watering and there is, of course, always some concern about possibly unacceptable results of watering on the 'going', e.g. very heavy rain following thorough watering makes for heavy going.

Regular mowing which encourages a relatively dense turf is decidedly important. Gang mowers with the height of cut set appropriately are normally used. Occasional fertilizer dressings are needed, using perhaps a granular containing 10% N, 15% P_2O_5 and 10% K_2O at 375 kg/ha (3 cwt per acre), but care is needed so as to avoid a lush growth which is likely to fall flat and create a peculiar thatch problem. It is usually important to include in the management periodic scarification of some kind to restrict the formation of a flattened layer of moribund grass which restricts grass growth. Spiked harrows are frequently used and quite often when there is much laid grass a machine resembling a hay turner does a better job than more conventional turf scarifying machines. As with all sports turf areas lime may be needed sometimes but it should not be given without the backing of soil tests.

Probably the biggest problem in maintaining a racecourse is providing the labour for 'tracking', i.e. divoting after racing. Damage from horses' hooves is considerable, particularly if the course is wet when used – the going soft. So far the best way of restoring the track is the labour–intensive one of having numbers of staff dealing with the situation manually. Torn up turf is replaced by the most convenient means (e.g. with forks or rakes) and stamped down while deep hoof marks are filled in with soil/sand/peat/seed. Consideration should also be given to complete overseeding from time to time over the years. This can be done in various ways but the Contravator approach is a very good one.

Rolling is required to restore surface smoothness and to firm up soft places resulting from repair work so as to provide safe and fair conditions for the next use. In the course of a year a considerable amount of rolling (usually ring rolling) may be required and frequent aeration with suitable machines is necessary to help drainage.

Take–Offs and 'Landings' at the Jumps

On National Hunt Courses these areas need a considerable amount of repair at the end of the season. Thorough spiking is needed to loosen the compacted soil followed by topping up level with extra top soil of suitable quality and sowing down preferably with a good hard–wearing cultivar of perennial ryegrass only.

Parade Ring and Lawns etc.

It must not be forgotten that horse racing is a spectator sport and that the parade ring and the various lawns on the course are a great attraction which need to stand up to a great deal of wear as well as look good on race days. Even the car parks must present a pleasing appearance!

RECORDS

In an era of highly expensive labour and materials sound budgeting and detailed accounting are vital needs for the successful management of all types of playing area. A suitable bank of information should therefore be compiled and maintained in order to assist both ground staff and administrators as much as possible in planning for requirements, making valid comparisons with past needs and in preparing budgets for the future.

From suitably kept records it is possible to assess the effectiveness of any operation carried out, evaluate the performance of labour, machines, fertilizers and chemicals etc. as well as gather information useful in forecasting replacement needs for equipment and machinery. Expenditure of time, fuel and cash can readily be accounted for thereby giving all-round satisfaction to everyone concerned.

Key to Recording

A site plan which shows dimensions of all areas under management is a fundamental background to all other forms of recording. Such a plan should also indicate buildings under supervision, drainage systems (including depth, outfalls etc.) irrigation systems and natural features. If kept up to-date-this facilitates quick reference and is of considerable use in the ordering and preparation of correct amounts of material for application to given areas etc.

Daily Records

A strongly–bound quarto or foolscap size diary or book allowing a page per.day is the basic need for daily recording. Information entered in the diary should cover all significant matters such as work and operations carried out, by whom, time involved, use of fuel and machines etc. along with suitable notes regarding weather conditions. Other important items such as the order and/or receipt of goods, incidence of disease, results of treatments, absence of staff etc. should also be noted, together with any other information relevant to the site concerned which may be of future value.

These daily records should be as complete as possible, yet precise and of simple format, i.e. easily read and understandable, for such material is of far more use than extremely detailed and complicated data. Continuity is also important and if the 'Recorder' is absent for any reason a predetermined deputy should always be available to carry on.

Permanent Records

From an efficiently kept daily diary one can readily produce summaries on a weekly, monthly and yearly basis for handy reference and for permanent records. There are numerous ways of doing this but such data is generally best understood when given in the form of concise tables. These should be prepared to cover individual local circumstances and tabulated to show whatever information is required in the long term, e.g. man-hours, machinery, fuel and materials as well as the application of materials and equipment to individual areas. Detailed information is advisable on various matters such as what fertilizers, fungicides, seeds and top dressings were used at what rate and when. Also on permanent record should be the areas of individual pitches and greens and information on machine settings, calibration of sprayers and distributors etc.

Duplication of the records is advantageous so that one copy can be retained for quick reference and one filed for executive purposes and long-term retention.

Visual Aids

A camera can also be a most useful supplementary aid to efficient recording. 'Before and after' colour pictures can be extremely helpful in many ways, providing valuable visual evidence. There are, in fact, many occasions when a good photograph might clear up an intricate point which would otherwise be difficult to explain or possibly lead to discussions of considerable length. When taking photographs it is helpful if a card or slate with date and site particulars can be included in the picture together with some familiar object such as a coin or a foot rule to indicate scale. Information about the picture should also be written on it *immediately* it is received.

In the production of all types of playing surface, modern requirements and demands call for a very high degree of technical and practical competence. This competence and all that it entails should not only be seen but also be placed on record.

N.B. Records of drainage alterations and drainage plans are particularly valuable.

RENOVATION AND RUNNING REPAIRS

Regular running repairs are necessary on most turf areas and it is in some ways unfortunate that it is the *best* sports turf which usually gets most attention in this respect – this being one of the reasons it is the best sports turf.

Major renovation work, which comes at the end of the main playing season, is much reduced if as much restoration work as possible has been done during the playing season. There are, of course, other advantages from keeping up with repairs, e.g. if a particular cricket pitch is renovated when it is finished with for the season, perhaps in July, then it has more time to re-establish before it is needed again.

Detailed attention to renovation work is given for each sport separately.

RESEARCH

The first turf research is claimed to have been conducted in Connecticut in 1885 but the world's first turf research station was

Three wear machines currently being used in research on durability of turf.

established in Britain in 1929 – as the Board of Greenkeeping Research (now called the Sports Turf Research Institute) at Bingley, Yorkshire.

Turf research is now conducted in many countries in the world but generally suffers from lack of financial support. This is certainly true in the U.K. where the amount of money available for research each year represents a remarkably low percentage of the annual expenditure on amenity turf construction and management (which is of the order of £150,000,000 or more).

An unfortunate characteristic of research is that there seldom seems to be an end to the need for it – as each problem is investigated it reveals other related problems about which there is little information. The Institute at Bingley has existed for nearly fifty years and achieved quite a lot despite paucity of funds. It has conducted useful trials on:

Moisture control for sports turf (especially drainage, including slit drainage)
Grass seeds mixtures
Cultivars of turfgrasses
Seed bed preparation and sowing
Fertilizer treatment
Mowing practices
Grass growth retardants
Weed control
Disease control
Pest control
Soil aeration
Soil warming to prevent frozen pitches
Testing turf for durability

All have contributed usefully to the pool of knowledge available on turf culture in the U.K. Despite this, despite the work done in other countries and despite the small but very useful amount of work done in some British universities in recent years, there is no doubt that there are vast gaps in our knowledge and that money spent on a great deal more turfgrass research in the U.K. would be money well spent.

Early season rolling to prepare for first-class cricket.

ROLLING

There is a story (well known but probably apocryphal like many of the best stories) that an Oxford gardener when asked by an American tourist how he produced such good college lawns said 'Well, we cuts 'em and rolls 'em and rolls 'em and cuts 'em for hundreds and hundreds of years.' This was a rather deflating reply and not quite correct – one can make a good lawn in less than two years and to roll a lawn regularly year in and year out is likely to result in a bad lawn rather than a good one.

Damage to Soil Structure

The roller, in fact, by applying pressure to the soil squashes the soil crumbs together and destroys them so that air is excluded and the free downward passage of water from the surface is disturbed. Drainage becomes poor and the grass plant suffers because the roots can not get enough oxygen to grow and develop properly.

175

Rolling a wet soil does more damage than rolling when the soil is relatively dry and, generally speaking, the heavier the roller the greater the damage to the soil structure, although one must take into account not only the weight of the roller but also its width and diameter when assessing the actual pressure imposed.

Lawns are not rolled much

A good lawn, then, is usually a lawn which is not rolled at all. This fact seems to be more widely accepted by home owners these days, to judge by the relative scarcity of garden rollers.

Rolling is needed for some sports

Where turf is used for sport and is not purely ornamental a smooth and in some cases hard surface must be maintained if games are to be played successfully. To obtain these conditions the roller must be used with discretion and, in order to overcome the bad effects of rolling on the soil, plenty of spiking and/or forking must take place.

Below, the various sports are listed in relation to the type and amount of rolling required:

Cricket tables

True fast wickets are needed and they can not be obtained without rolling (although many other factors are also involved in producing good wickets). On County grounds at least two rollers ('light' and 'heavy') are needed but the average cricket club can make do quite well with a single roller of a weight somewhere between 500 kg and a tonne (10 cwt and a ton). When the weight can be varied by adjusting the ballast this is ideal. Roller–pushing is not popular on cricket tables these days and therefore the roller must be powered by an engine. The table should be rolled well but not too well; rolling is done to get good wickets – not because of the pleasure of riding on the roller!

The best system of rolling is probably to firm up the whole table by repeated rolling in the early spring before the start of the cricket season, timing the rolling so that it is done when the moisture content of the soil is just right; then during the season rolling the actual wicket strips only as they are prepared for play.

176

Tennis courts

Here also some rolling is needed if good playing conditions are to
be achieved. Rolling on the average club court need not be as
heavy as on a cricket square. Quite often if one of the large motor
mowers (760 mm – 914 mm [30 in – 36 in]) is used to mow the
court an occasional run–over with a roller not exceeding 500 kg
(10 cwt) is all that is required.

Bowling greens

A hard surface is not needed here and heavy rolling is most
undesirable. Rolling just to settle back the surface after the winter's frosts is usually needed in March or April and then an
occasional light rolling during the season as necessary. No roller
used on a bowling green should exceed 250 kg (5 cwt) and special
bowling green rollers mounted on a wide frame which spread the
weight over a relatively large area are to be preferred.

If a bowling green is too soft the answer seldom lies with extra
rolling. Very often it is a question of extra scarifying to reduce the
amount of soft fibre at the surface and/or possibly a change in the
top dressing material (more sand being included for instance).

Golf greens

Correct top dressing is the real agency by which smooth resilient
(though not too soft) putting surfaces are built up. Rolling is
rarely necessary especially nowadays when quite weighty mowers may be used instead of the old light hand mowers. The first
cut with the mower in the spring may be enough to put back the
surface after the winter but a preliminary light rolling is sometimes useful.

Association Football Pitches

Maintenance of a smooth surface on soccer pitches throughout
the playing season is essential and this is not easy in the later
stages when the turf may have been cut up and parts of the pitch
have become grassless and muddy. After each game the surface
must be smoothed out again otherwise there is a risk that it will
freeze in the rough post–match condition, and then if the temp-

erature remains below zero the pitch will not be fit for the next game. A wide roller of wood or cast iron weighing just 50 – 100 kg (1 or 2 cwt) and pulled by hand is often adequate for smoothing back the surface. Special motorised light rollers are also useful. Frequently adequate rolling is accomplished through the use of the motor mower with the cutter held clear. Heavy rollers should never be employed on soccer pitches under any circumstances. Sometimes in certain conditions light flat harrows or fairly strong rakes can be used instead of light rollers for smoothing out the surface after a game.

Hockey Pitches

A smooth surface is essential on hockey pitches and sometimes a roller may prove necessary if the surface becomes badly cut up by play. Often, however, an annual roll in the spring with a wide tractor-drawn or tractor-mounted roller may be plenty, especially if supplemented by the pressure which one of the bigger motor mowers exerts. Hockey is often played on cricket outfields which may in any case get a rolling in the spring with the tractor-drawn or tractor-mounted roller. The cricket table roller should not be used on the outfield except, of course, where it has to travel over the outfield to get to the square.

Rugby Pitches

Rugby pitches do not need to be all that smooth and usually there is little need to roll them.

Racecourses

On racecourses a lot of rolling, especially where the course is on a heavy clay soil, is likely to lead eventually to poor drainage and soft going. Periodic rolling helps to smooth out the turf, however, and rolling of the National Hunt courses when the season finishes is usually an essential part of the renovation work. Cambridge ring rollers are particularly useful. Racecourses must be kept smooth and much good work can be done after a Meeting by a squad of men going round the track systematically topping up hoof marks with a soil/sand/peat/grass seed mixture and carefully treading back divots.

SAFETY AND SAFETY REGULATIONS

Familiarity breeds contempt and this unfortunately all too often applies with machines and materials used in turf culture. Care should be taken to minimise the possibility of injury by machines and all chemicals should be treated with the utmost respect and with due regard to the instructions provided – few chemicals can be claimed to be completely harmless. Known poisons should be kept in a locked cupboard and their labelling kept in good order. Protective clothing etc. should be worn as appropriate.

The Health and Safety at Work etc. Act 1974 applies essentially to all persons at work and imposes duties on employers and employees (even the self-employed are covered) to safeguard as far as is reasonably practicable the health, safety and welfare of the worker and of those who may be affected by work activities. There are many leaflets and booklets available on safety matters. They include:

'The Safe Use of Poisonous Chemicals on the Farm'	produced by the Ministry of Agriculture, Fisheries and Food.
'Farm Safety'	
'Health & Safety at Work etc. Act 1974. The Act Outlined'	produced by the Health & Safety Committee.

Whilst the new 'umbrella' act above is of primary importance safety regulations under previous specific safety acts such as the Agriculture (Safety, Health and Welfare Provisions) Act 1956 and the Factories, Offices, Shops and Railway Premises Act remain in force.

SAND

Sand is widely used to achieve physical improvement of soils prior to turf establishment and of top dressings for several types of established turf. It is sometimes used alone as a top dressing

179

for winter pitches but is seldom recommended without admixture for fine turf areas.

A suitable sand for the above purposes has a narrow particle size range and there is evidence that the most suitable sands (i.e. medium sands) have particles within the range 0.5 – 0.125 mm, a high proportion of these particles being of approximately the same size. A sand with a wide particle size range is inefficient as the particles will pack closely together. If the sand contains a high proportion of very fine particles these will tend to block the pores and the sand will give little improvement in soil conditions. Sands with a high proportion of large particles should also be avoided as these are less efficient than medium sands in compacted soils. Coarse particles can also cause problems as they tend to remain on the surface of the turf and may damage mowers and be unacceptable to players.

The sand used should be stable and not break down readily. Normally it should also be lime-free as, even when there is only a small lime content, when large quantities of sand are added the pH of the soil may be unacceptably increased.

For use in slit drains a wider choice of sands is possible – usually much coarser sands are more suitable but again they should preferably be lime-free.

Bunker Sand

There is no recognised specification for bunker sand in the U.K. but the accepted U.S.A. specification for such sand – one with a particle size range 0.25 mm–1.0 mm – is a good guide to requirements.

N.B. Avoid confusion with 'Lawn Sand' (which see) which is usually a preparation of chemicals and sand used, for example, for moss control.

SCARIFICATION

Scarification is an essential cultural operation for turf which is done by means of a rake or other device with a view to producing a healthy vertical type growth of the desirable grasses so as to improve the playing surface and appearance.

Fine Turf

Very light scarification (e.g. with a drag brush) is used simply to bring up recumbent foliage of the grasses in the sward so that it can be mown off leaving the turf perceptibly smarter looking. It helps to control the nap or grain which forms on some types of turf and which affects the run of a ball. Rather more searching scarification gets out of the turf dead and dying parts of the grass plants (mainly leaves and stems), thus letting in air and encouraging new growth. It also brings up stolons both of creeping grasses and of creeping weeds like white clover so that they can be mown off.

Unwanted grasses such as Yorkshire fog have leaves which tend to lie flat below the cutter and scarification, by bringing the foliage up to the mower, results in this grass being less conspicuous. Really severe scarification tears out much of the surface growth of Yorkshire fog and considerably weakens the plant to a point approaching elimination.

Many seed heads of annual meadow-grass grow very close to the ground and light scarification or brushing helps to bring a large proportion of these within reach of the mower with a view to reducing the spread of this grass.

Many fine turf areas are likely to suffer from an excessive production of fibrous material at the surface (see FIBRE – EXCESS AND CONTROL) and scarification is a big factor both in prevention and in cure.

General Sports Turf

Scarification of general sports ground turf is concerned with many of the same problems as are met in fine turf but with different degrees of emphasis. There is seldom a problem with excess fibre on a football field but there may be on hockey pitches, golf fairways and racetracks. On the other hand there is often a lot of dead plant remains to get out and, of course, really severe scarification can be used as a method of preparing a seed bed for renovation.

A selection of scarifying machines arranged to show their working parts.

Equipment Used

A wide range of equipment is available. Drag brushes and wire rakes are hand tools which are very useful for light work on areas which are not too large. There are wheeled wire rakes for manual operation and rake attachments for powered mowers.

Powered equipment is in widespread use particularly for fine turf areas. Such equipment typically involves rapidly revolving wire rakes or sets of blades mounted on a machine which resembles a motor mower. Indeed such a machine with knives which cut the turf vertically (instead of horizontally as in ordinary mowing) may be called a 'verticutter' and the work it does 'verticutting'. The powered implements can be adjusted to give very light treatment or to bite deeply into the sward, the latter being necessary when attempting to eliminate excess fibre. Where triple greens mowers are employed for golf greens special vertical cutting units are also provided to give the latter effect.

For use on larger areas similar equipment is avilable for use behind tractors but chain or spiked harrows are still of considerable value in many circumstances – for winter pitches, for golf fairways and for racetracks. When there is a considerable amount

182

of laid grass in a racetrack sward which is cut no shorter than about 150 mm (6 in) then a hay turner type of machine can prove very useful.

When to do it

It is important to integrate scarification into management with due regard to user requirements in each sport and to grass growth. Details of timing and frequency of scarification for the various types of sports turf are given under the appropriate headings.

SCREED

A screed is a very useful tool for flat bowling green maintenance. There are various home made devices but the basic model consists of a 3.05 m (10 ft) length of 32 mm (1¼ in) angle iron attached to a similar length of 50 mm × 25 mm (2 in × 1 in) timber and with a handle attached. The screed is drawn across the green to which top dressing has already been applied or with continuous feeding of the top dressing to the face as it advances. The screeding operation may be to repeat in different directions and on successive days until the top dressing has been almost completely 'lost', any surplus material being removed from the green.

SOIL

I. SOIL CONSTITUTION

Top Soil and Sub-Soil

The soil scientist distinguishes between various layers or horizons in the soil. For practical purposes it is usually sufficient to distinguish between top soil and sub-soil. The top soil is com-

183

paratively rich in plant foods, organic matter and bacteria etc.: the sub-soil is short of all these and may usually be regarded as comparatively barren. The sub-soil has, however, a considerable influence on the fertility of the top soil and the playing characteristics of the turf, particularly through soil moisture relationships.

In natural soil are found mineral matter, organic matter, soil moisture and soil air.

Soil mineral matter is formed through the breaking down of rocks by means of processes known as weathering of which there are two types – physical and chemical. Soil mineral matter consists of various sized particles varying from stones and fine gravel, through coarse and fine sand to silt and to the very fine particles of clay.

Different scales of particle size fractionation are used by different people but the one adopted many years ago by the International Society of Soil Science is still widely used. On this scale particle size groups are distinguished as follows:

Fraction	Diameter limits mm
Coarse Sand	2.0–0.2
Fine Sand	0.2–0.02
Silt	0.02–0.002
Clay	less than 0.002

Soil organic matter arises mainly from dead vegetation and is the home of countless micro-organisms such as, for example, the various bacteria concerned with nitrogen. Most of the organic matter is found in the top few inches – the top soil. Underneath lies the sub-soil containing little organic matter and usually lighter coloured. The organic matter contains a proportion of recognisable plant remains; the remainder, being dark coloured structureless material, is known as humus.

Soil moisture is an important constituent. Grass must have moisture at its roots. Mineral nutrients dissolved in the soil moisture are absorbed by the roots.

Soil air is necessary for roots to breathe and affects chemical and biological processes in the soil.

For healthy plant growth there should be a proper *balance* between mineral matter, organic matter, moisture and air.

Soil texture. Soils are classified into sandy soils, loams, clays etc., by the proportions of the various sized particles contained – sand, silt and clay; also organic matter. A true 'clay' soil has over 35% by weight of its mineral matter as clay particles, with less than 45% sand and less than 45% silt. A true 'sand' should have over 85% sand but can have up to 15% silt or 10% clay. Since the size of a primary particle does not change (apart from changes brought about by the slow process of weathering) the texture is an unchanging property of a soil. In practice soil texture is recognised by such characters as the feel of the soil when smeared in the hand, its stickiness when wet, its droughtiness in summer or the strength of its dry clods.

Soil structure. Normally in soils the primary particles do not exist on their own but are assembled together into aggregates. The binding together of particles is brought about by complex interactions between the soil particles, organic matter and various chemicals in the soil; the manner in which the particles are assembled is referred to as the soil structure. Thus, a soil may have a 'single-grain' structure typical of soils with little or no clay (and particularly some impoverished upland soils) in which there is practically no binding between the particles. A 'massive' structure is typical of some sub-soils in which the particles, although bound together, are in a close-packed arrangement. A 'crumb' structure is typical of good top soils, particularly those under grass, where the soil particles are clustered into granules or crumbs with large pore spaces between. The large inter-granular pores allow the rapid movement of water and these large pores become air-filled as water drains from the soil. The smaller pores within the aggregates remain water-filled when drainage ceases and thus a well-structured soil provides both air and water for the plant roots and soil organisms.

Pore space. Soil moisture and soil air between them fill the spaces between the solid particles of soil – the pore space. In natural soils the amount of pore space depends mainly on the soil structure – the better the structure the more pore space available. Under many sports turf conditions soil structure is destroyed, leaving little total pore space for air and water and restricting their passage. Hence the emphasis on the use of lots of suitable sand to ensure pore space despite compaction.

II. SOIL ACIDITY

Since the degree of acidity (or alkalinity) of a soil has such a considerable effect on the quality of the turf and of the playing surface it is not surprising to find it a subject of considerable interest to greenkeepers and groundsmen. The soil reaction (the degree of acidity or alkalinity in terms of hydrogen ion concentration) is presented on the pH scale which technically ranges from pH 0 (very highly acid) to pH 14 (very highly alkaline). With natural soils in Britain the range is usually from about pH 4.0 (very acid) to pH 8.0 (very alkaline). In chemical terms neutrality is about pH 7.0 but for all turf purposes a soil with a pH of 6.0 can be considered practically neutral and at this pH turf grasses (including perennial ryegrass) grow satisfactorily.

There is a tendency to over-emphasise the importance of pH in turf management – if the turf is performing satisfactorily it may be considered unnecessary to adjust the pH, whatever its value! The 'best' pH does indeed vary with the kind of grasses grown and the purpose to which the turf is put. For inland types of fine turf a pH between 5.0 and 6.0 may be considered satisfactory while for perennial ryegrass swards on heavily used football fields the pH should be held at about 6.0. Very good turf on some seaside golf courses is growing at pH's decidedly higher than pH 6.0 and so is the sea-marsh turf which is still so popular for making bowling greens. It is considered unwise to take positive steps to reduce the pH in these special cases, rather attempts to maintain it should be considered.

In general, soils grow more acid with time owing chiefly to natural losses of lime by leaching, these losses being increased by

186

atmospheric pollution leading to acidification of the rainwater and by the effects of some fertilizers. In time, therefore, soils may become too acid to support even the most acid tolerant fine grasses satisfactorily. Appropriate applications of lime (which see) are then necessary but liming should not be undertaken rashly (i.e. without prior soil test) since it can have such deleterious effects. A slightly acid soil discourages worms, weeds and diseases – increasing the pH removes the restrictions!

III. SOIL FERTILITY

Soil fertility may be defined as the ability of a given soil to grow satisfactorily some or all of the crops permitted by the regional climate. For turf purposes the 'crop' is, of course, grass and it may be noted that the word 'satisfactorily' appears in the definition. The need is *not* for maximum yield.

There is more involved in soil fertility than a good supply of mineral plant nutrients. It is worth noting, moreover, that soils contain a considerable proportion of the required mineral nutrients in *unavailable* form – they are 'fixed' in the soil – and the grass can make use of the *available* nutrients only. Further the standard plant foods supplied in fertilizers are only three in number – nitrogen, phosphorus and potash. These are undoubtedly the main ones needing attention but several other elements are also needed from the soil, e.g. magnesium and this may be of particular importance on 'artificial' soils containing a high proportion of added sand.

The lime status of the soil is important. Most turf grasses will tolerate a slight degree of acidity but over-acidity affects plant food availability and makes for an unthrifty turf; it may eliminate some of the wanted grasses. Over-alkalinity is also detrimental; it may make some mineral nutrients unavailable and it usually encourages common weeds, weed grasses, diseases and earthworms.

Soil structure is of considerable consequence affecting, as it does, root development, aeration and moisture movement. Good aeration favours the activities of favourable microorganisms in the soil. Grass roots need air and must have sufficient moisture without excess so that the ability of the soil to regulate these things matters a great deal. A good structure depends, amongst other things, on the soil having a suitable content of clay and/or organic matter. Both of these also affect the moisture and plant food holding capacity of the soil.

Soil temperature is obviously very much affected by the weather conditions but it is also affected by various soil characteristics, e.g. a very water retentive soil is much slower to warm up in the spring than is a drier soil and, of course, grass growth is influenced by soil temperature – there is not much growth below about 5.5°C (42°F).

Soil fertility can be seen to be quite an involved subject. In turf culture the aim is not maximum fertility to give maximum yields and some degree of *controlled* fertility is indicated. Attention to the desirable physical attributes of the soil to give good aeration and moisture control is often more important than generous fertilizer treatment.

IV. SOIL IMPROVEMENT (PHYSICAL)

The use of sports turf, especially during the unfavourable wet conditions which occur on many winter games pitches, leads to compaction of the surface soil and destruction of the soil structure. Unless action is taken to counteract these effects the movement of water through the soil may be greatly hindered, leading to wet surface conditions which will further increase the susceptibility to compaction and destruction of soil structure. Wet pitches can soon become mud baths and unacceptable for play and are likely to require major renovation at the end of the season. It does not matter how good the piped drainage system may be, if the water can not get through the top few inches of soil it will remain on the surface giving wet surface conditions.

The Problem

The major portion of the soil is made up of mineral particles which vary in size from the very small clay and silt particles to the larger sand and gravel particles. Normally in soils the ultimate particles do not exist on their own but are assembled together to form aggregates, the manner in which these aggregates are assembled or arranged being referred to as the soil structure. The formation of aggregates is brought about by the complex interaction of organic matter, various chemicals in the soil and the soil particles.

A soil has a good crumb structure if the aggregates are about the size of lead shot. Between the aggregates there are large spaces or pores through which water can pass rapidly and so air can enter into the soil. A good soil structure maintains a good balance of air and water in the soil giving rise to good soil aeration. During use, and even during routine maintenance procedures, the surface soil of sports turf can become excessively compacted and the soil structure may be severely damaged or even destroyed. When this occurs the aggregates are broken down and the large pores between the soil aggregates disappear so that water and air are unable to pass through the soil rapidly. In soils which have been severely compacted the ultimate particles are packed between each other, sand between gravel particles, silt between sand particles and clay between silt particles, so that any pores remaining in the soil are microscopic ones between the clay particles. Such pores conduct water extremely slowly and because of their small size are usually full of water and there is little space for air in the soil A surface cap of compacted soil will also prevent air from reaching the deeper layers of the soil where compaction is not so severe.

With compaction the structural profile, which would allow rapid movement of water and give a good water:air balance in the soil, is destroyed and a textural profile is left. Most natural soils have a wide particle size range and a high proportion of fine particles. The very small pores in a compacted soil of this nature are unable to conduct water rapidly. This type of textural profile is, therefore, unable to provide rapid movement of water and a good water: air balance in the soil.

A Solution to the Problem

Ideally every effort should be made to maintain a good soil structure, but this is very difficult under many sports turf conditions. Mechanical aeration is of considerable assistance in helping to keep soil structure and in promoting movement of water and air but there are limits to what can be accomplished in this way and physical amelioration of the soil is being increasingly adopted.

To allow rapid movement of water through a soil in which the structure has been destroyed the pores between individual particles must be large enough to conduct water rapidly. By improving the soil texture, such as by adding sand, the size of the pores can be increased. A considerable quantity of sand may be necessary to ensure that the fine particles of the soil (the silt and clay) are diluted so that there are insufficient to fill the pore spaces between the sand particles. The fine particles then have little influence on the way the soil behaves.

Soils used on areas such as football pitches, bowling greens and golf greens are frequently improved by the addition of sand. Ideally this is done during the initial construction but if not done then, by repeated top dressings later. On football pitches pure sand top dressings can be used as the sand quickly becomes incorporated into the soil by the action of the players and by renovation work. On fine turf areas, where play is less vigorous, it is unwise to apply top dressings of any pure material as layers may be produced which cause breaks in the rooting system and in moisture penetration. The sand should, therefore, be applied in sandy composts. Very few natural soils are sufficiently sandy as not to benefit from amelioration with sand.

Soils used for cricket wickets come into a different category because a high clay content is required to bind the surface of the wicket. Application of sand to cricket wickets is, therefore, not often recommended!

Type of Sand

The sand used for soil improvement should ideally have a narrow particle size range and it is suggested that the range should be that of medium to fine sand, 0.125–0.5 mm. The sand should preferably be lime free. The 'ideal' sand is not always available locally so that one resembling it closely may have to be used and sieve tests on samples of the sands available are necessary to guide the choice.

190

The Amount of Sand to be used when Constructing new Turf Areas

The amount of sand used in soil mixtures is critical. If insufficient is added little, if any, benefit will be gained. If too much is used then there could be increased problems of moisture and plant nutrient retention. The amount of sand to be added should be determined by laboratory tests on the actual materials to be used and the recommendations accurately adhered to.

Type of Soil to be used in Mixtures

The sandiest soil available should be used as it will require less sand to be added than will a heavier soil. Heavy textured soils also give problems during mixing as large lumps of soil tend to remain unaltered and the finer particles may ooze out on to the turf surface later during play in wet weather. In practical terms one can not easily produce a satisfactory mixture from a heavy clay soil.

The Use of Peat

Adding large amounts of sand to a soil to improve its drainage properties can have some deleterious effects. The water holding capacity of the soil is decreased, possibly leading to severe problems in drought. It is usually recommended that water is made available for areas with soils of this type. The addition of peat or other suitable organic material to the mixture increases its water holding capacity and also helps to retain more plant nutrients. Peat also has an added benefit in increasing the resilience of the new turf.

The peat used should not contain a large proportion of fine particles as these will block the pores created by adding the sand. A fibrous peat will tend to keep the mixture more open and help to increase the resilience of the new turf.

V. SOIL STERILISATION

Sterilisation, or more correctly, partial sterilisation, is a very useful way of eliminating unwanted weeds, diseases and pests

191

from top dressing materials such as compost or top soil and from the seed beds produced for fine turf areas such as golf greens. It may be accomplished through either heat or chemical treatment.

Heat Treatment of Top Dressing

Heating to 82° – 100°C (180° – 212°F) and holding there for a short time is very efficient. This may be accomplished by:

I. Dry Heat

Electric heating is done by introducing heating elements into the body of the soil or by passing a current through moist soil which when heated dries and cuts the current automatically. The former is preferred and is both efficient and economical.

'Baking' with solid fuel is often quite cheap and convenient though carelessness can easily lead to over-heating the soil and consequent damage. In this the heating is accomplished by means of hot flue gasses passing below a trough containing the compost. It is not difficult to construct a brick steriliser. For a steriliser of, say, 3 m³ (4 cu yd.) capacity, fuel required is about 100 kg (2 cwt) coke and 50 kg (1 cwt) coal dust. Compost sterilised by dry heat finishes in good condition for application to turf but unless great care is taken in the baking, the layers nearest the flues may be burnt and those further away not sufficiently heated.

II. Wet Heat

Steam sterilisation is comparatively simple and may be done with low or high pressure steam, the latter being usually preferred. There is no risk of over-heating but wet soil is liable to result if care is not exercised. The steam can be used to heat the soil directly e.g. by surrounding the soil with steam which then passes through it, or indirectly from perforated pipes in the bottom of the container.

An adequate steam generator is required for high pressure steaming and a locomotive type boiler can be used to give steam at 400–550 kN/m² (60–80 lb per sq in) pressure through 25–40 mm (1–1½ in) pipes.

Low pressure sterilisation is performed in apparatus consisting essentially of a fire beneath a shallow water tank below the soil container. Home made apparatus can be used for small scale work.

III. Equipment incorporating the features of dry and wet heat is available in which paraffin burners are used to heat a continuous flow of moist material down a revolving drum. Cheapness and speed of operation are advantages claimed.

Chemical Treatment

Various compounds have been used in the past (including carbon disulphide, naphthalene, formaldehyde [formalin], cresylic acid and chloropicrin) but they have been replaced in most cases by methyl bromide and dazomet.

Methyl bromide is a gas which is very toxic. It is an effective soil sterilant but because of its toxicity its use is limited to experienced, licensed persons. In turf culture its use has been mainly in the preparation of weed-free seed beds. The soil needs to be reasonably moist and soil temperature should be at least 10°C (50°F). The rate used is usually 70g/m² (2 oz per sq yd).

Dazomet (Basamid) is a material which can be used fairly easily as the product is sold as granular prills which release a gaseous sterilising compound on contact with water. The soil must, therefore, be moist for successful results. For sterilising seed beds dazomet is used at 380 kg/ha (340 lb per acre) for light – medium soils (heavy soils, silt soils and soil high in organic matter (e.g. peats) may need a higher rate (570 kg/ha or 510 lb per acre). The material has to be incorporated by means of a rotary cultivator, preferably through the top 180 – 200 mm (8 – 9 in) of the soil. Dazomet can also be used to sterilise soil heaps at a rate of 170g/m³ (4½ oz per cu yd).

As with methyl bromide, the treated soil has to be covered with a polythene sheet to trap the gas. After sterilisation has occurred, the period required being variable and depending partly on soil temperature –which should be at least 7°C (45°F), the soil must be ventilated before any use is made of it. Samples can be taken and used in a cress growing test to check that the removal of the gas is complete. Good, but not 100%, control of weed seeds can be achieved.

Methyl bromide is more expensive than dazomet but the job can be done in a shorter time with it. This does, however, involve the employment of a specialist contractor and if it is desired to use one's own labour then dazomet is the material to choose.

NOTE. Safety precautions are important when the toxic chemicals are being utilised and electrical equipment should have high safety standards since electricity and moisture from the soil can otherwise provide a fatal combination!

VI.   SOIL   TESTS

A.   *Chemical Tests*

Occasional routine laboratory analysis (say every three years) of soil samples for pH and available plant foods can be of considerable help in turf management. The results of the tests need expert interpretation and they are only valid if the soil samples are fully representative of the areas sampled. When sending samples for test the following points should be observed:
1.   Each area to be tested should be reasonably uniform. If it is otherwise, then more than one sample is required.
2.   Most turf users have a hollow tine fork which may be used as a sampling tool. From 50 to 60 cores should be taken from various points of the area concerned and mixed together to make one sample.
3.   When sampling large areas like playing fields or unsown land a spade or trowel may be used, but a large number of sub-samples is still required.
4.   Each sub-sample (or core) should be as near 150 mm (6 in) deep as possible.
5.   The amount of soil sent for analysis should be about 0.5 kg (1 lb) per sample — no less. If a much larger amount is obtained, e.g. when sampling with a trowel or spade, the soil should be well mixed on a clean floor and a sub-sample sent in.
6.   Each complete sample should be placed in a suitable container such as a strong polythene bag.
7.   The sample (or samples) should then be securely packed in a strong container (e.g. of wood) and, if separate samples are put in one box, care should be taken to see that they do not

become mixed. Each sample should be furnished with a separate clear label which should be on wood, good stiff card or other stout material and not on flimsy paper. A good black pencil is better than pen and ink for writing the label since ink tends to run if the label becomes moist as it often does when packed with damp soil or turf. Indelible pencils or ball points should not be used. The name of the sender, source, purpose, etc. should be stated as appropriate and a covering letter sent separately to indicate requirements.

B. *Physical Tests*

Physical tests on soil samples, such as mechanical analysis to determine soil texture or hydraulic conductivity tests, are seldom required for existing turf but are frequently of value when constructing new turf areas. Sampling procedures etc. should be generally as described above but greater quantities of soil are required, e.g. 1.0 kg (2 lb) for mechanical analysis, 5.0 kg (10 lb) for hydraulic conductivity tests

STORAGE OF MATERIALS AND EQUIPMENT

There are very few sports turf areas where good and secure storage facilities are not essential.

Modern turf management involves the use of much expensive equipment for which clean, dry and safe storage space is very necessary. If the accommodation is furnished with engineering tools and electricity (for power and lighting) so much the better.

Safe, dry storage is also required for various materials including fertilizers, weedkillers, fungicides, wormkillers, grass seeds and top dressings. These tend to have special individual requirements and account needs to be taken of this in storage – as well as of the importance of not allowing inter-contamination and of preserving the labels with the packages!

Bags of fertilizer can be stacked flat on a wooden pallet to avoid unnecessary contact with a damp floor and to allow air circula-

Switching fine turf with glass fibre tipped switch.

tion. They should not be stacked on end or dropped on their corners because of the risk of splitting. Weedkillers, fungicides and wormkillers should be kept apart from the fertilizer and from each other and should be locked up for safety reasons. Grass seeds should be kept away from all the above materials but should be kept free from damp in a cool and airy place.

Top dressing is a bulky material which may not need the same refined accommodation as other materials but prepared material does need to be kept dry so that it is ready for immediate application when wanted.

SWITCHING

Switching is very useful for rapidly dispelling dew and used regularly can do much to prevent disease attack on fine turf by providing a dry surface. A dry surface also helps good mowing as well as being liked by players. A switch can also be used for

196

scattering worm casts when they are in dry condition. Originally it consisted simply of a 4.5–6 m (15—20 ft) bamboo cane mounted on a suitable handle. Switches with flexible but strong steel wire then became popular but most modern switches are probably made from replacable fibre glass rods about 2 m (7 ft) long mounted on a handle which may be aluminium tubing fitted with handle grips.

TOP DRESSING

Top dressing is the application to the turf surface of a bulky material chosen chiefly for its physical attributes. Suitable top dressing improves levels; it encourages root growth and drought resistance; it serves as a protection for newly-sown grass; it promotes better surface drainage, and – perhaps most important of all – it can provide the special kind of surface needed for a particular kind of sport.

Materials

On fine lawns, bowling greens and golf greens the best material for top dressing purposes is usually a friable sandy compost. On many golf courses 'real' compost is manufactured from heaps consisting of alternate layers of soil and rotted organic material such as farmyard manure. After standing at least a year such heaps are broken down and the compost then mixed with an appropriate amount of sand and passed through a fine screen before use.

Where facilities for compost making are not available substitute mixtures of sand, soil and organic material such as fine granular peat or leaf mould are used, e.g. 6 parts medium sand, 3 parts sandy soil and 1 part peat. When surface conditions tend to be too moist and airless a proportion of a material such as granular wood charcoal may be useful in the top dressing.

For cricket tables the top dressing should be such that when moist it will roll out flat to give a firm cohesive surface which

197

provides a satisfactory degree of pace and bounce and which possesses suitable lasting properties. A heavy loam soil free from grit is usually suitable and on county class wickets it would seem that an even heavier soil, e.g. a clay top soil, is becoming more popular. Where the available top soil is not sufficiently heavy in texture it may be improved by mixing with it a proportion of marl, e.g. 20%.

On heavily used tennis courts the kind of top dressing required is more comparable with that of cricket tables than with that of bowling greens. Heavy loam soil helps to produce a hard wearing surface giving true bounce.

The requirements of golf tees are somewhat different and often a very sandy mixture is appropriate on these areas. Similarly on football and rugby pitches, etc., a sand/soil mix may be useful although in some circumstances sand alone often proves to be of most value.

When dealing with fine turf areas it is important to avoid applying materials which produce definite layers in the soil beneath the turf. Many troubles have been caused by top dressings of pure sand, for example, which in the course of time have become buried and caused a break in the continuity of moisture penetration and of the rooting system.

When to apply

Application of top dressing should be related to the state of grass growth as well as to the needs of play and intensity of use. On fine turf areas the most convenient time is usually at the end of the summer but before growth ceases since if top dressing is applied when there is no growth there is risk of damage through smothering and disease invasion. There are of course circumstances where light top dressing during the summer months may be appropriate.

On winter games areas top dressing with sand during the playing season is quite common. Such applications are also made during renovation work as well as during the summer months.

How to apply

Spreading is generally done quite satisfactorily by a shovel in the hands of a skilled man but mechanical spreaders are available.

Mechanical spreading is probably more common on winter games areas but can be restricted by the quantity of material required and the effects of this on the weight of the equipment when loaded. When the surface is soft the gross weight of a machine and its load may do more harm than the top dressing does good.

All materials should be suitably screened – usually 5–6 mm (3/16 – ¼ in.) – and be in a dry condition when they are applied. With fine turf areas particularly, the surface on which they are spread should also be relatively dry.

Working in

The process of top dressing is not ended when the material has been spread. On fine turf areas working of top dressing into the surface by suitable equipment is most important. On golf greens this may be accomplished by a drag mat or drag brush. These implements (more particularly the drag brush) are also used on tennis courts, bowling greens and cricket tables but many groundsmen prefer to use some kind of lute on cricket wickets. Indeed a special lute may be used on all these areas. On winter playing pitches working in may sometimes be left to the players but frequently chain harrows or drag brushes are needed.

Sterilisation

Partial sterilisation of soil or compost used for top dressing aims at eliminating weeds and harmful organisms and there is much to commend this treatment. It is difficult to arrange, however, and is, therefore, infrequently done, reliance being placed on selective weedkillers to eliminate any broad–leaved weeds which might result. Possible trouble from weed grasses etc. is conveniently overlooked.(See SOIL STERILISATION).

Organisation of Top Dressing

Compost heaps need to be built ahead of the time when they are going to be needed. Top soil, sand etc. need to be ordered in good time and they are usually purchased on the basis of a sample. Last minute efforts can lead to serious disappointment. Late delivery could also mean that the material arrives just when it is wanted

199

but in a wet and unsatisfactory condition for application. It is best to get delivery well ahead of requirements and to have appropriate storage accommodation so that the material can be suitably screened, prepared and kept in satisfactory condition ready for use when wanted. Only a small amount of equipment may be needed for preparation but suitable screening tackle is essential while mixing is easier if there is a concrete floor.

TREES FOR USE OF GOLF COURSES AND SPORTS GROUNDS

Choice of Varieties

Many new sports grounds are being constructed which provide large areas of grass unbroken by any planting and open to all the winds. It is more pleasing to see a well treed site with the trees forming a background to the sports ground and blending the area in with the surrounding landscape! This may not be possible immediately on a new sports ground but a tree planting scheme should be incorporated in the design so that there is provided for posterity something other than a strictly utilitarian series of pitches. On new golf courses it is usually possible to leave many established trees but supplementary planting is frequently needed in addition. When considering tree planting the design should take into account the species of trees indigenous to the locality so that the ultimate scheme blends with the existing landscape. For this purpose deciduous forest trees are generally most suitable with some conifers interplanted. Soil types will also have to be taken into consideration and here again a careful study of the surrounding tree population will serve as a useful guide to the species which are most likely to succeed. It is of course necessary to site trees carefully in relation to pitches, golf greens etc. because, desirable as trees are, they are liable by shading, leaf shedding etc. to interfere with the production of good turf playing surfaces and their roots may get into drains.

Industrial Areas

In industrial areas where there is fairly high atmospheric pollution deciduous species will thrive more readily than conifers. The shedding of their leaves in late autumn and their dormancy during winter (when there is highest atmospheric pollution) is considered to be of importance in the resistance of deciduous trees to pollution. The following species have shown remarkable tolerance of polluted conditions and can be considered for sites within industrial areas:

Tilia × *euchlora*	Lime
Platanus × *hispanica*	London Plane
Acer platanoides and varieties	Norway Maple
Acer pseudoplatanus	Sycamore
Crataegus monogyna and varieties	Hawthorn
Sorbus aucuparia	Mountain Ash

Exposed Sites

Exposed windy sites may cause difficulty when designing a planting scheme because many species will not tolerate exposed positions. Among those which will withstand such conditions are:

Acer spp. particularly *Acer pseudoplatanus*	
Crataegus spp.	Hawthorn
Betula verrucosa	Silver Birch
Alnus glutinosa	Alder
Fraxinus excelsior	Common Ash
Quercus pedunculata	Oak
Pinus sylvestris	Scots Pine
Pinus pinaster	Maritime Pine

Favoured Localities

In more favoured localities the tree planting can be much more ambitious with consideration given to spring and autumn effect of the leaves, e.g. larch in spring provide a wonderful colouring with new foliage and some species of *Acer, (griseum, platanoides Schwedleri, plantanoides Reitenbachii), Quercus (coccinea)* and *Crataegus (crus-galli)* give a beautiful autumn colouring.

Very pleasing effects can be produced which will enhance the site and fulfil practical purposes as shelter belts and screening.

Planting on Golf Courses

The value of tree planting has been appreciated to a far greater extent on golf courses than it has been on sports grounds. In addition to providing a 'setting' for the course trees can be used for distinguishing fairways and on some occasions for directing the line of play.

Soil types again play a large part in determining the species to be used. Forest trees can be used as the backbone for the planting scheme with suitable shrubs interplanted.

On the acid, peaty courses Rhododendrons and Azaleas can be used to good effect in association with Silver Birch, Brooms and Gorse.

Probably the most difficult courses for planting are the coastal ones exposed to the sea breezes. Some of the pines will probably prove useful on such courses *(Pinus pinaster, P. sylvestris* and *P. radiata)*; sycamores are often blighted by salt spray but they battle on and generally survive with considerable success; willows such as *Salix alba* and *S. caprea* can often be relied on and *Ulmus glabra* – Wych Elm has withstood very exposed coastal areas. Shrubs can play a useful part and the Sea Buckthorn – *Hippophae rhamnoides* is an obvious choice. Gorse is another valuable shrub and *Olearia* × *haastii* and *O. phlogopappa* are also much used. When there is a little shelter *Berberis Darwinii* and *B. stenophylla, Escallonia* varieties and *Hosta* varieties will generally succeed and add interest to the planting scheme.

Obviously the above lists of trees and shrubs are not intended to be comprehensive and many other subjects of equal merit could be added.

Siting

Greens. There is no doubt that trees are the making of many a golf course, both as decoration and as making a positive contribution to the design of the various holes. When planting around greens the ultimate height and spread of the trees at maturity should be borne in mind, especially if only specimen trees are to be planted. Good turf can not be maintained in heavy shade even during the summer; shade encourages disease and winter shadow from trees on the south and west sides of a green may mean that the turf is much more susceptible to damage caused by play on a frosted or partly thawed surface.

Tree roots will spread into well watered and fertilized putting green turf with alacrity so that often the side of a green nearest to trees or shrubs is weak and unthrifty through loss of water and nutrients. Roots also have an affinity for drains – it is necessary to be especially careful to avoid planting on or near drains or the main drain outlets. In general trees should never be closer than 10 m (11 yds approx), shrubs 2.5 m (2½ yds approx). to the edge of the putting surface. Young saplings and shrubs will grow almost imperceptibly, sometimes among older trees and when a green becomes shielded from direct sunlight and free air flow by a deep semi-circle of trees and woody shrubs the turf becomes very susceptible to fusarium patch disease. Such a green will be much healthier if the growth of the young trees and shrubs is drastically thinned out. Conifers are better avoided near greens since the shed needles which are very difficult to remove from the turf surface may have a detrimental effect on the grass.

Tees. Similar remarks apply to tees. A tee will never do well sited in a tunnel of tree branches; the grass becomes thin and weak while, in the winter especially, the surface is soft, never really drying up.

Any tree branches actually overhanging the edge of a green or tee should certainly be pruned back. Rainwater dripping from the branches and twigs directly over the turf thins out the grass and encourages moss and surface slime moulds. The extra moisture may also encourage fusarium patch disease.

Fairways/Rough. Tree planting within the actual fairway areas is seldom undertaken and it is, in fact, difficult to establish young trees in such situations. However, established trees, or small groups of two or three, may be incorporated into the design of a new hole very effectively. Single specimen trees or small groups

203

can often be used in the semi-rough to define the turn at a dog-leg hole and 'direct' play.

Larger groups of trees and plantations should be confined to the rough. Wtih 'forestry' type plantations of young trees rabbit proof (even deer proof) fencing may be needed for any chance of success, and the requirement for regular clearing around the young trees in their early years and the thinning at intervals later on must be kept in mind.

Sports Grounds. Planting of such areas can be extremely effective but it is dictated to a large extent by pitch layout. Group plantings can make use of awkward corners which would be unused otherwise and are preferred to single lines of trees. Shelter belts can enhance both the beauty of the site and the comfort of users and spectators. To be really effective a good width of planting is necessary with, say, a stout hawthorn hedge on the boundary at the windward side, a line of deciduous trees, then conifers and a final outer row of deciduous trees. On graded sites embankments can be planted with groups of trees and shrubs such as broom or hawthorn.

Great care should be taken to plant in such positions as to avoid root encroachment into the drainage system.

Leaves

The splendid colour and variation of autumn leaves may increase the enjoyment of participants on sports field or golf course, but they do cause problems for the maintenance staff. A cover of leaves, particularly when waterlogged, must never be left for any length of time on turf since if it is, the turf underneath becomes thin, pale, spindly and disease prone. Small mechanical leaf sweepers will quickly remove leaves from greens and similar areas. There are also larger tractor mounted models suitable for dealing with fairways, rough or winter pitches.

Leaves do have their uses — they can be built up in layers with soil into compost heaps. When fully rotted, the material can be screened and mixed with sand if necessary to make a first class top dressing.

Maintenance

On most golf courses and sports grounds autumn and winter are the seasons when some time can be devoted to the maintenance of trees and shrubs. It is usually best to establish a planned programme that will fit in with the rest of the winter routine, rather than wait until an emergency arises

Evergreen shrubs

Generally evergreens – rhododendrons, *Berberis darwinii* etc. do not need pruning at all in a systematic way. Work may be needed occasionally to improve their shape or prevent them becoming over-large. If these shrubs become thin and lanky they may be improved in vigour and density by more severe pruning back to older wood and this is best done in early spring just before new growth starts.

Autumn flowered heaths also benefit from pruning (or a light trimming with shears) in the spring before growth has started. However, it is wise to avoid cutting back into wood more than about 2 years old.

Deciduous shrubs

A good general rule for these subjects is to prune in the season that will allow the fullest period of growth before the next flowering season comes round. However, on a golf course or sports ground some compromise may have to be made. Since time is at a premium in the summer some pruning jobs that should properly be completed at that time may have to be deferred until the winter.

Shrubs that flower on current season growth like *Spirea varieties* and *Buddleia davidii* generally blossom at the end of the summer and their pruning can be safely left until autumn or winter. Where the shrubs have attained the size required the year's growth may be cut back hard to within a few buds of its base. Small specimens need only the ends of the shoots removed. A few very early flowering shrubs come into this category, e.g. forsythia, which is pruned immediately the flowers are over and before new growth starts.

Shrubs that flower on the previous season's growth should not be cut back as described above in winter since to do so would be to remove all the flowers. Ideally growth should be thinned out in summer after flowering, i.e. stems that have borne flowers should be cut out or pruned back to vigorous new growth so as to let in light and air, allowing proper ripening and development of the new shoots. If the job is held over until the winter care should be taken to cut out old flowered wood, only pruning back to strong new growths, preferably fairly low down. New growth is often quite easy to spot, the young bark being a brighter, cleaner colour and, of course, these stems will not have the remains of flowers/seed heads attached.

Basic pruning

The work should be carried out in an orderly fashion bearing in mind the following points:

(a) Removal of dead, diseased or injured and broken parts should be given first attention.

(b) On large shrubs the next step might be to remove several of the older stems, low down or at ground level. This will help stimulate new productive wood throughout the plant.

(c) Attention to maintaining the overall shape and form natural to the subject being dealt with is important. Crowded or crossing branches rubbing, as well as branches and twigs that do not fit the natural outline should be picked out.

When branches cross or crowd it is usually necessary to remove one or more of them, bearing in mind how the remaining branch will affect the look of the plant: it may be better to remove both crossing branches from that particular location. Similarly where many branches are crowded together they should gradually be thinned out until a good balance is achieved with the rest of the plant so as to achieve a uniform density.

Pruning cuts

Equipment should be in good working order and adequate for the job at hand. Hand secateurs may be expected to cut satisfactorily branches up to 12.5 mm (½ in) diameter; above this long-handled loppers or pruning saws are more appropriate.

206

All cuts should be made flush with a large stem or back to a lateral growth, avoiding the leaving of stubs. Subsequent growth in the required direction is encouraged by cutting back to a suitably placed twig or bud. A clean cut, sloping away from the intended direction of growth should be made, approximately 6 mm (¼ in) or so above the chosen twig or bud. Larger cut surfaces should be pared clean with a sharp knife and painted with a proprietary wound dressing such as Arbrex.

Young trees/plantations

Young plantations neglected in summer should have weed and grass growth scythed and removed in autumn, taking the opportunity to replace any failures. Staked trees should be examined for loosened stakes, ties rubbing and corrective measures taken. Specimen trees planted to dictate line of play are vulnerable, particularly when young, to damage or loss of the leading shoot which could detract from their appearance when mature. If such damage occurs the main stem should be cut back to a strong bud, and a suitable replacement leader selected from re-growth. In many cases it may be practicable to cut back to an existing secondary shoot, temporarily staking this to encourage upright growth for a year or two and tipping back any shoots or branches of equal vigour.

Young trees growing in areas where it is desired to keep the grass regularly trimmed and neat can have lower branches gradually removed over a period of years to a height of 2 m or so (6 or 7 feet) to ease mowing operations. This practice would also be quite acceptable where trees are to dictate line of play on a golf course since the bulky canopy still presents a problem to the golfer and the clean tree stems aid maintenance and location of lost balls.

Mature trees

Regular pruning is not normally needed and when required it is usually a specialist job. Things to watch for are holes or crevices in major limbs (which can lead to rot establishing) and dead or storm damaged branches that present a danger.

TURF NURSERY

Particularly for especially important turf areas such as bowling greens, cricket tables, golf greens, golf tees and tennis courts a well maintained nursery of suitable replacement turf is of great value for the repair of areas damaged by wear, disease, accident or vandalism. It is appreciated that a suitable space is not always available but wherever it is possible to have one the value of a turf nursery should not be overlooked.

The preferred position is one that is easily accessible and within reach of the hydrants, possibly adjacent to the storage sheds used for machinery and materials. The site should be well prepared and have a cover of stone-free soil (to facilitate lifting) matching the areas for which the turf is intended. Sometimes turf is used in constructing a new turf nursery but usually establishment is effected by sowing suitable grass seed, the mixture sown being selected to match the area being catered for. Initial preparation, fertilizing etc. should be on normal lines.

In practice, preparing a turf nursery is a relatively straightforward matter but there is greater difficulty in ensuring the regular first-class maintenance which is so essential if the nursery is to serve its purpose of providing good replacement turf at short notice.

Usually nursery turf established from seed needs about two years before it is entirely satisfactory for replacement purposes so that a suitable size for a nursery is twice the estimated annual requirement *plus* an amount for contingency!

VEGETATIVE PROPAGATION

In the U.K. turf is usually produced from sod or seed and rarely from stolons. In the United States and in other parts of the world vegetative production of turf is very common; it also occurs to some extent in southern Europe.

Vegetative methods of turf production are normally limited to those grasses which produce an abundance of creeping stems. In this country this means creeping bent or velvet bent but in warmer climates other grasses such as Bermuda-grass may be used. Various creeping types of turfgrasses which produce only small amounts of seed are also grown vegetatively in appropriate climates, e.g. St. Augustine grass, Centipede grass and Zoysia.

The success of the vegetative method is based on the ability of the creeping stems to root at the joints and produce new plants. A little information on the method may be interesting though it is of little practical consequence in the United Kingdom at the present time.

Preparing the Ground

Thorough preparation of the land to produce conditions similar to those of a good seed bed is required and usually some fertilizer. A guide to the amount of stolons required can be obtained from the following alternative suggestions:

100 – 200 litre/100 m² (2–5 bushels per 100 sq yd approx.)
1 m² of stoloniferous bent to 10 m² (1 sq yd to 10 sq yd approx.)
500 – 1,000 g stolons/m² (1–2 lb per sq yd approx.)

Planting

The procedures for planting stolons vary with the size of the area to be planted, with the type of material available and with the sort of equipment that can be obtained conveniently.

On small areas the alternative procedures are:–

(a) Chop the stolons into short lengths about 50 mm (2 in) long and scatter these lightly like chaff on the prepared bed. They should then be top dressed heavily with soil and lightly rolled.

or

(b) Take complete stolons and plant in rows 100 – 150 mm (4 – 6 in) apart.

On a larger scale a common method is to spread the complete stolons or, more usually, 150 mm (6 in) lengths of stolons over the area, then to run over the area with a special machine like a disc harrow with blunt discs to push the stolons in and finish with a roller to press them in. It is usual to top dress afterwards quite heavily. For large areas adapted row planters have also been used in the United States.

Even in this country it is surprising how quickly a planted area will produce a turf if it is well looked after. An area planted in September can almost be good enough for a putting green by June the following year. A supply of water is essential to keep the stolons moist before and after planting.

Planning Ahead

Careful planning is needed, of course, when organising the planting of stolons. These can not be allowed to sit around very long since they deteriorate quite rapidly and are subject to disease.

Obviously a first requirement if one wants to go in for planting stolons is a supply of good stolons and these are not readily available. In fact, in practice in Britain it is almost essential to start one's own turf nursery in advance – if one can find a good variety of creeping bent to start with. For such a nursery a good sandy soil that will shake loose is an advantage. A one metre row of stolons in the nursery could produce enough stolons in a season to plant 130 m² (150 sq yd approx.). Alternatively, one square metre of stoloniferous turf broken up and planted out will grow a crop of stolons sufficient for planting several thousand square metres.

Some Pro's and Con's

One advantage of vegetative propagation is the uniformity of the turf which it is possible to produce — if one starts a nursery with a single plant the final area produced will have a turf all produced from the one plant. The fact that the grasses used are stoloniferous does, however, have the disadvantage that the turf may be particularly liable to produce a mat or thatch of surface fibre unless carefully managed and on a golf green it may, like a billiard cloth, have a nap influencing the run of the ball.

In the British Isles vegetative production is seldom used because in our climate creeping bent is normally regarded as inferior to browntop bent for the production of fine turf such as golf greens. If creeping bent is wanted there is now available seed of good cultivars. (See GRASSES)

WATERING

Introduction

The average annual rainfall for the British Isles is over 1.09 m (43 in) and this is spread quite well through the year. In these circumstances it is not surprising that in the British Isles watering of turf does not receive the same attention (practical and scientific) as it does in warmer climates with lower and less well distributed rainfall.

The Need for Irrigation

The general picture, however, does not tell the full story – the average rainfall for dry areas, like East Anglia, is less than 640 mm (25 in), whilst that for the wet, mountainous areas of Wales is over 2.03 m (80 in). Moreover, whilst there is quite good distribution throughout the year it is by no means perfect, dry periods occurring in March, May, June, the beginning of July and the month of September.

The potential loss of moisture by transpiration during the summer is between 60 and 75 mm (2½ and 3 in) per month on average, according to district. Thus in dry areas in dry months, when the rainfall may be down to 12.5 mm (½ in) or less, the soil is very likely to dry out to the point where grass roots are unable to obtain sufficient moisture to make up for transpiration losses, and there is a case for artificial watering if colour, appearance, texture, growth, suitability for use, etc. are not to suffer. This is particularly true on closely mown turf which usually has shallower rooting than less intensively maintained turf and, therefore, is dependent on a smaller volume of soil for its moisture supply.

211

In the past many groundsmen and greenkeepers were reluctant to water for various reasons and there is some justification for this attitude. On fine turf areas at any rate this reluctance has largely disappeared with the demand for higher quality, good looking turf all the year round and there is an increasing acceptance that on such areas *judicious* watering can be beneficial. Serious drought conditions in Britain are, however, relatively rare and those without water can do a great deal to minimize the effects of drought through such management practices as top dressing and raising the height of cut in very dry weather. There are many situations where watering of less fine turf is regarded as advantageous, e.g. for encouraging recovery of renovated winter pitches. In circumstances where there are specially constructed turf areas, which are almost entirely composed of sand, it may be necessary to apply irrigation regularly, even daily.

Apart from the direct benefits to the turf of ensuring sufficient supplies of moisture to prevent deterioration, an efficient irrigation system facilitates other aspects of management, making it much simpler to arrange fertilizer application, weedkilling, scarification, etc.

The Effect of Watering on the Turf

To maintain satisfactory top growth and colour in turf there must be sufficient soil water in the root zone. A deficiency of water results in stress and if this is allowed to persist for more than a few days wilting occurs and the turf will develop brown spots. In time some of the grass will die, but such extreme circumstances are rare in Britain.

Stress occurs whenever the rate of water loss by transpiration from the leaves exceeds the rate of water intake through the roots. Thus stress may occur when there is a reasonable supply of water in the soil if, for any reason, the root system is inadequate. For example, there could be insufficient root available to absorb water quickly enough at high temperatures. Shallow rooting can be related to management practices, including over-watering. Root growth depends on the soil conditions including drainage, grass species, mowing practice, irrigation management, aeration, etc. Irrigation management which keeps the soil near saturation constantly, will restrict aeration and rooting depth.

212

Near the surface some aeration is, of course, available from the proximity of the atmosphere so that surface rooting is encouraged. The grass roots tend to develop mainly in the mat or thatch above the soil surface because of the better aeration there. When a large proportion of the grass roots are in the mat the turfgrass may require watering every day in drought conditions. This means, in turn, constant wetness and more surface root – the problem feeds upon itself. As these conditions encourage root growth in the mat or thatch the depth of fibre increases and becomes a distinct problem in overall turf management.

When soil physical conditions are favourable roots will penetrate deeper if irrigation management provides water only as needed, without excessive applications, and where there is time in between waterings to allow partial drying.

It is believed that some golf clubs have been persuaded to install watering systems because of a marked lack of drought resistance of their greens in situations where this was not primarily due to a lack of water *per se*, but due to an excess of fibre and shallow rooting. In view of these remarks it is clear that if we have a fibrous mat problem to begin with, watering may make it worse, especially since the mat itself is water holding and tends to impede percolation of water down into the earth. With or without a watering system it is still necessary to eliminate the excess of fibre and obtain better rooting.

Some grasses are known to be more drought resistant than others; thus fine fescue is relatively resistant to drought and annual meadow-grass less resistant. Constant heavy watering is likely to reduce the proportion of fine fescue in a turf and to increase the annual meadow-grass content.

The Influence of Soil

Soil consists of solid particles with spaces, called pores, between them. In the pores are held the water and the soil air that are necessary for grass to flourish. If all the pores are full of water, the soil is saturated, there is no air present and the development and activity of roots are stopped. Initially water in the soil drains from the largest pores where it is not very firmly held, and air fills the spaces thus created. After drainage has ceased the soil is said to be at field capacity – the remaining water is held somewhat

213

more tightly by the soil particles, thus preventing further drainage. Irrigation should not apply more water than is needed to restore the soil moisture content to field capacity; excess means wastage of water, possible waterlogging, plus risk of leaching of plant nutrients. At low soil moisture contents the water is spread as a thin film over the surface of all the soil particles. Medium or fine textured soils have a greater total particle surface area than coarser textured soils and thus they are capable of holding more water after drainage. On the other hand when the film of water on the surface of the particles gets very thin it is held very tightly, so tightly that it is not available to the plant. It is thus possible for a fine textured soil to contain more water than a coarse textured soil but still be 'dry' as far as the grass is concerned.

The entry of water into the soil (the infiltration rate) is markedly affected by soil type. The infiltration rate on a clay soil, perhaps 2.5 mm (0.1 in) or less per hour will be much less than that on an open textured sandy soil, possibly 12.5 mm (0.5 in) or more per hour, so that water could be applied much more quickly on sandy soil. Compaction, of course, also has a considerable effect. A compacted soil will be relatively slow to take in moisture. On cricket tables, with their compacted heavy soil, infiltration rate is low and so, therefore, is the rate at which water can be efficiently applied. It is always wise, of course, to arrange for an application rate lower than the general infiltration rate, to avoid saturation conditions and to avoid run-off from any areas that have a lower infiltration rate or which are on slopes.

Water Supply and Quality

The most common source of water is the mains supply; indeed, this may be the only supply for many sports clubs. Unfortunately, when water is most required there can be restrictions on its use for watering sports turf so that, where possible an independent source is well worth looking for, e.g. a well or river. (A licence is required from the appropriate River Authority to withdraw water from such sources). Alternatively, storage of mains water may have to be considered.

Cost needs to be taken into account when considering alternative sources of supply; main supplies usually attract a meter charge, storage costs money and private supplies usually involve extra cost for the provision of pumping equipment.

The main requirement for water is that it should be wet but, particularly for private supplies, where pollution is possible it is wise that a chemical analysis of a potential supply be carried out at different times of the year before spending money on a new watering system. A soft (lime free) water is to be preferred to a hard water; air warm water is better than icy cold water, but both of these are relatively minor points if the alternative might be no water at all when it is needed.

Capacity of Watering System

Ideally each watering system should be designed by an experienced water engineer but in practice systems are commonly designed by general consultants or by specialist irrigation firms. Obviously a new system must be capable of providing enough water and a useful guide to overall requirements is the equivalent of 25 mm (1 in) of rain per week, 254,000 litre/ha (22,600 gal per acre) to provide sufficient water to offset potential transpiration in periods without rain. This is an average figure, but it is possible to calculate a more exact requirement for a particular area from weather records and appropriate tables if necessary, adding half as much again to cover percolation losses, drift losses, uneven application etc. On large schemes it is clearly unnecessary to water all areas at once so some discussion is required between the customer and the designer on how the load should be spread and, of course, regard must be paid to the rate of application.

Irrigation Equipment

In this country there are still people who water with a hose pipe with a rose on the end, but this is not highly recommended. Most people have watering systems based on conveniently placed hydrants from which a hose is taken to the chosen portable sprinklers. Sprinklers each have their own optimum working pressure and so the choice of sprinkler should ideally be taken into account with the design of the scheme. Uniform distribution is important from the point of view of best use of water and best results on the turf, but unfortunately uniform distribution is rarely achieved. A great many people use rotary sprinklers and with these, apart from the need to get uniform distribution within the circle treated, there is a further complication of trying to merge adjoining circles satisfactorily. For square areas like cricket squares, tennis courts and football pitches, spray lines are often preferred.

In the last few years, particularly on golf courses, increasing use has been made of fixed location pop-up sprinklers, but it is likely that other sports will follow the trend. There is obviously a great saving in labour with such equipment, and pop-up systems are made even more obliging if they are fitted with automatic controls, which allow the greenkeeper or groundsman to pre-arrange a watering programme to be carried out overnight if required, so as to give minimum interference with the use of the turf. Clearly, the easier watering is made, the more likely it is to be done when it is required but, unfortunately, there could also be an increased tendency to over-water just because it is so easy.

Irrigation Management

Whilst grass roots need moisture at all times a slight deficiency and some degree of stress is not always a bad thing – it allows air into the soil and encourages the roots to grow deeper, which is highly desirable. Moreover, a deficiency reduces risk of a subsequent excess from possibly unexpected natural rainfall.

Just when to water is essentially a matter of experience. Theoretically very exact control is possible through the use of tensiometers installed in the soil to give an indication of the available soil moisture, but we know of no practical use of such equipment in this country. A rain gauge can, however, give useful guidance. The greenkeeper or groundsman uses his experience – he may find help from probing the ground or from taking core samples to a depth of 150 mm (6 in) to examine the soil but often he will base his judgement on keen observation of known sensitive spots, which show up shortage of water before the rest of his turf and before anybody else has spotted that anything is wrong.

The amount of water given at any one application should aim at keeping moist the top 150 mm (6 in) or so and in drought con-

216

A selection of sprinklers with pop-ups in action in the background.

ditions this may need to be applied at, say, 2–3 day intervals (longer intervals in less droughty conditions), allowing a period between for the surface 50–75 mm (2–3 in) to dry out a bit and let in air. The frequency may have to be greater on light freely drained soils than on heavy, poorer drained soils. Frequent light watering may also be necessary to bring on areas seeded during renovation.

The rate of application of the water should not exceed the infiltration rate of the turf – water will penetrate quicker into sandy soils than into clay soils and quicker into uncompacted soils than into compacted soils. There is also the question of the mat or thatch, more particularly on golf greens and to a lesser extent on bowling greens, which can be very water repellent and water holding From many points of view an excess of fibrous mat at the surface is undesirable and it should be eliminated by management, including scarification. Water held in the fibrous mat encourages surface rooting and the production of more mat. The lack of deep root leads to the necessity for more frequent watering which leads to the condition getting worse. Over-watering leads to lack of aeration, lack of deep root development and also an increased susceptibility to disease. Where there is difficulty in ensuring adequate penetration of added water, spiking before watering can be of assistance. On some areas of turf there may be patches which, after drying out, take water with great difficulty and on these areas spiking is particularly important. In extreme cases a wetting agent may be used but there are disadvantages in these chemicals and they should not be used too freely.

There is often discussion as to the best time of day to apply water but there is little positive evidence that any one time is better than another. By and large it is believed that watering during the heat of the day is likely to lead to greater evaporation losses during application and to make the turf more susceptible to disease. Turf diseases are dependent on moisture so clearly watering is likely to have some influence, especially bad watering which keeps the turf wet all the time and/or keeps the soil saturated. Watering during the night or in the early morning, when the surface is normally moist anyway (and when it is often relatively calm) means that during the day the surface can dry out, thus reducing the time when surface conditions are moist and conducive to disease. Another aspect of the disease problem is the tendency for incorrect watering to encourage annual meadow-grass which is known to be particularly susceptible to fusarium patch disease. A dry surface during the day also usually means more suitable playing conditions and a reduction in the compaction effects of traffic.

There is a fairly common belief that turf which is irrigated needs more fertilizer, particularly nitrogen. This may be true where over-watering and heavy leaching take place but with good watering practice irrigation losses should be very low and it should only be necessary to increase fertilizer rates very slightly to make good losses from increased growth. Extra fertilizer (particularly nitrogen) is likely to create a need for more water – the start of a vicious circle.

WEED CONTROL

I. CONTROL OF BROAD-LEAVED WEEDS

The normal treatment for broad-leaved weeds

For broad-leaved weeds there is available a wide range of weed-killers based on the selective or growth-regulator herbicides. These are taken in mainly through leaves and, by a fairly slow process of upsetting the weed's growth processes, they distort and eventually kill the plant. The original and cheapest selective herbicides, 2,4-D and MCPA, are still widely used and are effective against many weeds, e.g. plantains and creeping butter-cup. More usually, however, 2,4-D or MCPA is blended with a herbicide from another more expensive 'family' – mecoprop, dichlorprop or fenoprop (previously called CMPP, 2,4-DP and 2,4,5-TP respectively). These increase the number of weed species which can be controlled. Mecoprop, for example, is more effective than 2,4-D or MCPA against pearlwort and white clover. Although numerous combinations are sold, the most widely used combination is 2,4-D and mecoprop. At a rate of active ingredient of about 1.1 kg 2,4-D plus 2.2 kg mecoprop per hectare (16 oz plus 32 oz per acre) this will give reasonably good control of most turf weeds and can be considered the basic herbicide treatment for turf, generally best given in spring or early summer. Ioxynil plus mecoprop is another valuable wide spectrum mixture.

Resistant weeds

Effectiveness of weedkilling depends on weed characters like hairiness or tap-root, maturity of plant, growing conditions and numerous other factors. Some resistant species, or particularly tough plants, require two or three applications, normally at intervals of 3–4 weeks. If the spring application and a follow-up treatment still leave one or two weed species unaffected, it is wise to check that these weeds are indeed susceptible to the herbicides being used. If MCPA or 2,4-D alone has been applied, using a mixture with mecoprop should be considered. If this mixture has

219

been used, then mecoprop alone, at a higher rate than in the mixture, or a different herbicide such as dichlorprop, dicamba or ioxynil may be necessary. These last have special value against certain weeds even though they are less suitable than mecoprop as general purpose weedkillers. Dicamba, for example, is especially useful against knotweed which can be a problem in areas that receive heavy wear, while ioxynil blended with mecoprop and applied in early spring before flowering is particularly useful against speedwells.

Effective application

Overdosing must be avoided. High application rates may defeat their own object by 'scorching' foliage and preventing complete intake of herbicide into all parts of the plant. Also there is danger to the turf. A moderate dose, repeated frequently, is most effective.

Applications should be made when weeds and turf are growing actively, i.e. generally from April to September, and preferably during fine warm weather when the soil is moist. The weeds

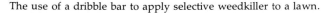

The use of a dribble bar to apply selective weedkiller to a lawn.

then respond quickly to the herbicide and the grass grows vigorously to dominate them and fill in. Treatments during drought are likely to damage the grass while heavy rain will wash the weedkiller off the plants and through the soil and thus render it ineffective. Short dry periods or light showers, however, are not likely to cause problems.

To ensure active growth, it is a good plan to link weedkiller treatments with fertilizer dressings during the summer, aiming to apply weedkiller a week or two after the fertilizer. Combined fertilizer/weedkiller preparations have some attraction for the domestic lawn owner.

A margin of time between mowing and spraying is desirable – preferably 2–3 days either side of spraying, but at the very least one day between spraying and the next mowing so as to give the herbicide time to be taken in by the weeds.

Selecting and diluting the herbicide

Choosing the right herbicide depends upon identifying the weeds present and then consulting an appropriate source to decide which type of product is most suitable. Rates of application should be those recommended by the manufacturers unless there are very special reasons for doing otherwise. Where it is required to apply other than the rates recommended by the manufacturer it is, of course, necessary to know the proportion of each active ingredient. It is recommended that in all normal circumstances use should be made only of products approved under the Agricultural Chemicals Approval Scheme.

The amount of water to be mixed with the weedkiller depends on the type of equipment used. Medium volume – 225-675 litre/ha (20-60 gal per acre) – is customary for sports turf. The lower the volume then the higher usually is the risk of drift.

The persistent problems

If weeds are still persisting after several applications attention to management may be indicated – for example drainage, changing the pH with lime or sulphate of ammonia, increasing fertility or changing height of cut.

221

Checking equipment

A possible cause of inadequate weed control, or alternatively of turf damage, is a discrepancy between intended and actual rate of application per acre. When was the sprayer last calibrated to check the volume of liquid applied to a given area at a given speed of travel? Have different nozzles been fitted since then or is a new man using the sprayer? Changes of this sort can appreciably affect application rates. It is worth spending an hour checking the application rate for each sprayer. Unless this figure is known reasonably accurately, careful choice of weedkiller and rate may be a waste of time.

If spray effects show up unevenly, the first thing is to check that all nozzles are working properly and that there are not overlaps or gaps between the spray 'cones' from the nozzles when they are at the normal working height. Working height may need adjustment. It is important also to make sure there are no misses or overlaps at application. The use of markers helps to ensure accurate lining-up and where possible, e.g. on small rectangular areas, applying the herbicide in two half-rate doses at right angles to each other increases efficiency of cover. If drift is a problem, it may be helpful to use nozzles that give larger droplets or – for small areas – to use a dribble bar or special fluted roller machine. (An ordinary watering can with fine rose may be the best choice for a small lawn.) Windless days should be chosen for selective weedkilling particularly on garden lawns but also on playing fields or golf courses.

New sowings

With weeds, as with other problems, prevention is better than cure. New sowings should be made as weed-free as possible. The most effective method is sterilisation of the seed bed with methyl bromide or dazomet, though this can only be considered for relatively small areas such as golf or bowling greens. Otherwise, fallowing the seed bed for as long as possible is desirable. A whole year is by no means longer than needed to get rid of weeds, though usually other considerations prevent so long a period. In fallowing, the land is worked down as near as possible to a seed bed and each crop of weeds cultivated out as it comes and before seed is set. To replace or supplement cultivation, paraquat or

222

Two forms of appliance for putting weedkiller on to turf: on the left a popular sprayer and on the right a machine which is used where drift is a problem, the weedkiller being applied by the roller.

diquat may be used: the former is better against grasses, the latter against broad-leaved weeds. They have a rapid contact action, and, most important, are inactivated almost at once after use so that sowing is not delayed. (The latest formal recommendation is to wait three days, though often a shorter period proves perfectly safe in practice.) Paraquat or diquat can also be used to kill weeds showing before the turfgrass seedlings emerge. Care is needed to make quite sure that the grass seedlings are not through the soil, and there is a possibility that seed on the soil surface may be affected though seed covered by soil should be quite safe.

Once the grass seedlings have emerged and have two or more leaf blades, it is generally safe to use ioxynil (without admixture with other chemicals) at 1.1 kg/ha (16 oz per acre) active ingredient and this will control a number of weeds provided they are still at the seedling stage. Morfamquat is also sold for use on seedling turf.

On fine turf sown with fescue and bent, it is best not to use the normal selective herbicides like 2,4-D and mecoprop until it is 'well established'; a sward sown early in spring might safely be sprayed after a good summer's growth, whereas one sown late in autumn should not be sprayed until the following spring. For

223

Weed spraying on extensive turf areas.

coarser turf spraying can be considered at an earlier stage. Rye-grass and timothy, for example, can generally·be treated without much risk with 0.84 kg/ha (12 oz per acre) of 2,4-D amine or 1.4 kg/ha (20 oz per acre) of mecroprop when they have two or three leaves; and higher rates, nearer the normal, could be used after the start of tillering (production of new shoots at ground level).

Resowing

When resowing areas in which weeds have been killed by herbicides, it must be remembered that some selective herbicides remain active in the soil for several weeks, particularly mecoprop. In rushed circumstances it may be necessary either to remove and replace about an inch of top soil or, at least, to increase the seed rate.

224

Control of Knotweed

Knotweed (an extremely hardy annual in many a football pitch) becomes more resistant to selective weedkillers the older it becomes, and therefore, if it is possible, the best treatment consists of spraying with a 2,4-D weedkiller when the young knotweed seedlings are just appearing in the thin or bare places in the pitch in spring. The main seed renovation can safely follow the application of 2,4-D in a day or two since this particular weedkiller (as distinct from most others) seems to be relatively nonpersistent in the soil. If, however, the knotweed seedlings are late (and seed renovation must follow immediately the end of the football season) then either one must use a suitable ioxynil product on the seedling turf or one must wait until the new grass can safely be sprayed with an appropriate selective weedkiller, preferably one containing dicamba, taking care with the dosage rate.

Final reminders

All treatments must be carried out with great care. With weedkillers more harm can be done in a short time without anyone realizing it than with anything else normally used by the groundsman. Not least, harm to the operator.

All herbicides should be treated as dangerous poisons: most of them are, especially in concentrated form straight out of the container. Care is needed in measuring out and mixing the concentrated weedkillers. The spray must not be inhaled and, as appropriate, gloves, protective clothing and face masks should be used.

Before opening any container it is essential to read everything on the label which should be carefully preserved. Containers require safe storage and careful disposal.

Hand Weeding

One of the safest and surest ways of selective weedkilling on a small scale is still that of removing the weeds with a small hand fork! An isolated weed in an otherwise clean cricket table or green should be taken out promptly before it spreads. There are still greens, cricket squares and lawns in this country (although admittedly not all that many) which as a result of a skilful general

225

management programme coupled with a modicum of hand weeding have yet to be sprayed with chemical weedkiller!

II. CONTROL OF WEED GRASSES

Particularly in fine turf, some grasses are commonly regarded as weeds. Under close mowing most of the coarser grasses such as are used for areas like football pitches fail to survive but any plants of these which do survive in such areas are, of course, weeds.

The two most common weed grasses, however, are the natural invaders, Yorkshire fog (*Holcus lanatus*) and annual meadow-grass (*Poa annua*). The former occurs in disfiguring patches while the latter, although it may start in patches, commonly spreads to mix completely with the existing sward and even to replace it almost completely. Indeed most fine turf areas contain a considerable amount of annual meadow-grass and there are those who would argue against its elimination! Heavily used winter pitches commonly have a great deal of annual meadow-grass which so readily colonises bare ground.

At the present time there are no chemicals which can be recommended for selective elimination of weed grasses in existing turf. If not too plentiful, patches of Yorkshire fog can be replaced by good turf and, where this is impracticable, sustained periodic severe scarification of individual patches will disguise the patches and may gradually reduce and eliminate them.

As regards annual meadow-grass good management plays an important part in reducing its spread. Important factors include regular scarification or brushing before mowing to bring seed heads up to the cutter, boxing off cuttings, and the use of the right kinds of fertilizer, e.g. avoiding those which raise surface pH.

III WEEDKILLERS FOR NON-GRASS SURFACES

On non-grass surfaces weedkiller may be needed to kill existing vegetation, to keep a clean surface free of weeds or to do both.

226

There are several types of herbicide; different types are generally combined to give weed control that is both complete and persistent.

Paraquat and diquat

Both these chemicals are excellent for a quick kill of growing plants, unless they have strong underground rhizomes or taproots. Paraquat is more effective against grasses and diquat against broad-leaved weeds. A mixture of paraquat and diquat is available for general weed control work. Doses range from 0.56 – 1.1 kg/ha (8 oz – 1 lb per acre) for regular maintenance against annuals and seedlings, up to 2.2 kg/ha (2 lb per acre) for well-established weeds. The herbicides act quickly on and through the leaves and there is virtually no persistence in the soil. They are, therefore, ideal to kill weeds on bare ground just prior to sowing and for use in bunkers and jumping pits from which sand is liable to be splashed onto surrounding turf. Paraquat will, however, remain active for some time in organic matter, e.g. in strings used as marking lines from which it can be released by rain when the strings are re-used. Paraquat and diquat can be used any time in the growing season.

Glyphosate

This is another herbicide which does not persist in the soil. Unlike paraquat, it is effective against grasses with rhizomes and therefore is potentially very useful for couch grass in bunkers.

Sodium chlorate

This herbicide is taken up by plants through leaves and roots. It kills existing vegetation quickly and, unlike paraquat and diquat, persists for some time in the soil to prevent establishment of seedlings. Doses for an initial kill of established weeds are 224–448 kg/ha (200–400 lb per acre): for preventing re-establishment of weeds 112–224 kg/ha (100–200 lb per acre). The higher doses normally persist for up to 6 months; the lower ones 2–3 months. Treatment can be made any time during the growing season, but higher doses are needed in early spring than in summer. Sodium chlorate can move sideways as well as down-wards in the soil and may damage plants including shrubs and trees adjacent to the treated area. Because of the fire risk from dry organic matter such as dead plants to which sodium chlorate has been applied, all Approved Products containing sodium chlorate are now mixed with a fire retardant.

Borax and other boron compounds

Boron compounds are root-absorbed and rather slow-acting. They are mainly used for keeping an area free of weeds; a dose of borax at $170 - 500$ g/m^2 (5 g – 15 g per sq. yd.) applied in late winter and early spring will prevent weed growth for a season. Boron compounds are quite easily leached from the soil but are very persistent if not leached and are, for example, used for pre-surfacing treatments under asphalt pavements.

Organic Residual herbicides

There are many herbicides which can persist in the soil for a year or more, according to dose and soil conditions. These include diuron, bromacil, atrazine, simazine, dichlobenil and chlor-thiamid, all of which are taken into plants mostly through the roots, although some can be absorbed through the leaves to some extent.

All these herbicides are generally best applied in late winter or early spring, just before the growing season. Insoluble ones such as simazine and diuron can also be applied in late autumn, although persistence is likely to be less than with late winter or spring applications. On the other hand, if application can not be made until the growing season has started, some of the more soluble herbicides – e.g. atrazine and bromacil – are preferable because they will move more quickly in the soil. These two have the additional merit, if weeds are already growing, of intake through the leaves.

None of this group of herbicides will move sideways to any appreciable extent on level, normally-drained ground, although they will of course do so if the ground is waterlogged and water lies on the surface. However, plant roots spread sideways, e.g. under a path beside a lawn, and may take in herbicide, especially with repeated treatments.

In general higher rates are needed on heavy or organic soils, on grounds made up with a layer of ash or cinders, in summer and in high rainfall areas. Lower rates are appropriate for light soils, late winter and early spring applications and low rainfall areas.

Miscellaneous herbicides

Some of the following are used in various situations, mixed with the herbicides already described or others for total weed control:

2,4-D; MCPA; 2,3,6-TBA; 2,4,5-T. Absorbed mainly through leaves and effective against broad-leaved weeds.

Picloram. Absorbed through leaves and roots; particularly effective against woody weeds and deep-rooted perennials; resists decomposition in the soil and is very persistent, therefore not in general use and should be used only with special care.

Dalapon and aminotriazole. Absorbed mainly through leaves, and slightly through roots; comparatively short persistence in the soil. Both are useful against grasses but aminotriazole is also used against deep-rooting broad-leaved weeds.

Creosote and mineral oils. Used to kill vegetation in small areas but are generally too unsightly and too unpleasant to handle for large-scale use.

Ammonium sulphamate. Taken in through leaves and roots; used specially against woody plants and well established broad-leaved weeds on concrete or asphalt paths; only short persistency.

The full range of Approved Products can be seen in the current Handbook of the Agricultural Chemicals Approval Scheme.

Weed control round trees and shrubs

Treatment with herbicides near shrubs or trees always needs care to check the safety for each species. Dichlobenil, simazine and diuron are useful for this purpose. The proper treatment for shrubs and trees is an extensive subject and if necessary reference should be made to specialist publications.

Paraquat is usually safe provided that it does not touch the leaves or the bark of young trees.

Moss on paths, hard tennis courts, etc.

Moss can be controlled by calcined sulphate of iron, at 17 g/m²
(½ oz per sq yd): by borax at 100–140 g/m² (3–4 oz per sq yd), or
by simazine, atrazine or diuron at 11 kg/ha (10 lb per acre).

Safety

All herbicides are dangerous to a greater or lesser degree,
especially in concentrated form. Paraquat has received publicity
because it is widely used and carelessness sometimes leads to
fatal results but all herbicides should be treated with respect,
even the organic residual herbicides which are of low toxicity
compared with some others. The fire risk with sodium chlorate
has already been mentioned.

IV. WEEDKILLERS – FURTHER SOURCES OF INFORMATION

Manufacturers give a great deal of helpful information on the
efficient and safe use of their products on their labels and in
leaflets. The latest (1977) booklet 'List of Approved Products and
their uses for Farmers and Growers' (produced under the
Agricultural Chemicals Approval Scheme of the Ministry of
Agriculture, Fisheries and Food) is very helpful and, of course,
the Sports Turf Research Institute has its own advisory leaflet
available for members.

Very full information on weed control (not confined to turf) is
given in The Weed Control Handbook published by Blackwell
Scientific Publications. The two volumes of the Handbook – Vol. 1 on general principles and Vol. 2 on detailed
recommendations – deal extensively with weed control and
give much information on herbicides and their effects on weeds.
It is important to consult the latest editions (currently 5th edition,
revised reprint of Vol. 1: 7th edition of Vol. 2).

WETTING AGENTS

Wetting agents are chemicals used to lower the surface tension of water. They are constituents of some fungicide and weedkiller spray products with the purpose of assisting the penetration and spread of the material being applied.

Special wetting agents may also be of value in assisting penetration of rainwater or water applied from sprinklers into very dry, water resistant patches of turf.

For some purposes ordinary washing up liquid may be suitable.

WINTER PITCHES *(Association football, Rugby football, Hockey)*

Playing Surface

Each of the sports wants a surface which is reasonably firm and dry but which will provide a satisfactory stud hold. Hockey demands a firm, fast and true surface so that when a ball is hit it does not readily rise in the air but runs freely on the ground. The grass should not be too long – 12.5–18 mm (½–¾ in). The ideal surface for soccer is not very different but slightly less true conditions are acceptable – the ball is much bigger. The favoured height of cut is about 25 mm (1 in). Rugby is probably the least demanding but reasonably smooth and 'dry' conditions are still well regarded. For Rugby a hard ground is not favoured and longer grass – about 50 mm (2 in) – is left on for the playing season.

Drainage

For good performance it is essential that heavily used winter pitches should have first-class drainage in the fullest sense. Clearly a great deal depends on the original construction of the pitches – whether they were handled correctly, provided with pipe drainage, given adequate soil amelioration etc. Once a pitch has become established some faults are difficult or impossible to correct but certainly an adequate pipe drainage system can and should be installed if there is not one already. Without this the groundsman is under a tremendous handicap unless the pitch happens to be on a very permeable sub-soil with a low water table. Spiking helps the water away from the surface but can be of only limited value if the water can not get any further. Slit drains also need outlets!

End of Season Work

Planning. If any major improvement works are to be done (e.g. pipe drainage or slit drainage) then detailed organisation for these should be started well in advance so that any contractor involved can move in as the players move out!

Renovation work must also be planned well in advance. All materials required, e.g. grass seed, fertilizer etc. should be ordered so as to be on hand at the appointed time. Failure to estimate accurately the quantities of grass seed required may on the one hand result in delays whilst acquiring more seed or, on the other, costly wastage of the excess. Everything should be ready for work to begin, weather permitting, as soon as the last match has been played so that completion can be achieved before the end of May if possible.

Soil Compaction. Even after a season of only moderately heavy wear, the soil at the surface of most pitches can be expected to be compacted. Spiking will of course have been carried out throughout the playing season but the period immediately prior to renovation offers the opportunity to spike really intensively. Spiking to offset compaction will also give the young grasses a good start by providing well aerated soil conditions which allow full root development and water penetration.

Weed Control. Where there is extensive renovation general weed control is generally best left until late summer when any new grass is quite well established but knotweed (*Polygonum aviculare*) may need special attention. If this annual weed produces seedlings in the spring before renovation starts it may be worth while

232

Specialised equipment for renovation reseeding – the Auto-Contravator/Lospred.

spraying it at this susceptible stage using a product based on 2,4-D only, since it is safe after using this particular weedkiller to seed about two days later. Once the grass seed is sown it is best to wait until the end of the summer when the grass is firmly established and then spray with a dicamba product. However, in severe cases of knotweed infestation there may be serious competition between knotweed and the new grass in its first weeks and in this case spraying with a product based on ioxynil alone may be carried out on the seedling turf (See WEED CONTROL).

Cultivation. For small scale work as in goal mouths, bare areas can be dealt with by using hand tools. Where more extensive work is required mechanical assistance, even including shallow ploughing, may have to be used. The use of rotary cultivators is not advised as these tend to produce a 'fluffy' seed bed and also a cultivation pan which can led to drainage problems. Disc harrows can be used on areas requiring renovation but which retain some grass cover, the angle of the discs being adjusted to provide the severity of cultivation required. The final tilth can be obtained by use of spring or solid tine harrows, chain harrows or a tilther rake. Specialised renovation machinery which, without prior cultivation being essential, drills the seed into narrowly spaced slits can be used with advantage on many areas. The importance of providing good conditions for the seed can not be over-emphasised.

Fertilizer. The whole pitch should receive a dressing of granular fertilizer which should be applied at least a day or two prior to sowing, and in fact, it is often advantageous to apply it before the playing season finishes so as to give as much encouragement as possible to existing grass. Unless soil analysis reveals a particular nutrient deficiency, a complete granular fertilizer containing nitrogen, phosphate and potash in suitable proportions is generally satisfactory, e.g. one containing 10% N, 15% P_2O_5 and 10% K_2O used at 375–750 kg/ha (3–6 cwt per acre).

Amelioration. Cultivation work provides an opportunity for amelioration of the soil where this is required. Incorporation of suitable lime-free sand, particularly in areas subject to puddling, can considerably improve drainage conditions. At the same time levels can be adjusted by making up hollows with sandy top soil or a sand/soil mix.

Sowing. The seeds mixture to use depends on the type of pitch involved. It is unwise to use poor, cheap mixtures in an attempt to economise since this invariably leads to unsatisfactory results.

For Rugby and soccer pitches one of the more persistent cultivars of perennial ryegrass can be used on its own. Most other grasses are unable to establish themselves adequately under the conditions prevailing and in the short time available; they are therefore of little use. For finer turf areas such as hockey pitches a mixture containing species like Chewings fescue, creeping red fescue, browntop bent and timothy is often used but the best new cultivars of perennial ryegrass should now be considered. For all grasses, only good cultivars should be used and all seed should be certified (See GRASSES).

234

The seed rate has to be adjusted according to the density of the existing sward on the areas to be renovated. On most types of pitch a maximum of 35 g/m² (1 oz per sq yd) should be allowed for where the ground is completely bare, with lower rates where some grass persists. Higher seeding rates should not be necessary if seed bed preparation is adequate and a good seeds mixture is used. This is particularly important with present-day seed prices.

Subsequent Management. It is essential that the young grasses should be allowed to develop unchecked by adverse conditions. In this respect watering is of major importance to maintain growth during dry weather, although over-watering should be avoided at all times. Before the first mowing light rolling of the renovated areas is often advisable to firm the soil around the young seedlings.

This first mowing should be carried out when the grass is about 60–75 mm (2½–3 in) high, removing no more than 25 mm (1 in) of growth at the first cut. It is particularly important for the first cut that the mower should be in good condition and that the blades should be keenly set. Further mowing should be carried out as often as grass growth requires.

Summer Management

To maintain good growth the desirability of watering in dry weather should not be overlooked. Further fertilizer (particularly nitrogenous) may also be required and of course regular mowing (boxing off cuttings if practicable) at the appropriate height, say, 25 mm (1 in) for soccer and Rugby, 20 mm (¾ in) for hockey. It must not be forgotten that a really strong cover of grass when the playing season starts is a tremendous advantage.

When conditions allow regular aeration and occasional top dressing with sand is usually advantageous.

Autumn and Winter Management

As the playing season approaches the height of cut should be regulated – a little shorter for hockey, rather longer for Rugby.

A very important aspect of management is maintaining and

improving drainage. During the playing season aeration by weekly mechanical spiking supplemented by hand forking helps to get surplus water away quickly, thus improving playing conditions and helping the turf to survive. Occasional sanding during the playing season is also useful in many circumstances. Rolling may be necessary from time to time to restore the playing surface but it should be kept to a minimum because of its adverse effect on the soil. The aim should be to use the lightest suitable roller as infrequently as possible. The use of chain harrows or similar equipment is sometimes more appropriate than rolling. Where practicable replacement of divots should be undertaken immediately after play since this will do a great deal to extend the 'useful' life of the pitch.

Good marking out sets off a good pitch!

WINTER PITCHES IN FROSTY WEATHER

In most winters a number of games of hockey, soccer and Rugby have to be cancelled because of hard frozen pitch surfaces. Unfortunately there is no cheap and easy solution to the problem. A good cover of grass is a great insulator and thus, despite the difference in requirements, Rugby pitches are probably less affected than hockey and soccer pitches because there is usually more and longer grass. Pitches can be prevented from freezing by means of insulating covers – if the cover is put on early enough. Various types of insulating blanket have been introduced with varying degrees of success but the old fashioned pitch insulator, straw, is still as good as anything. A pitch well covered with straw sufficiently in advance of the frost can be relied upon not to freeze in any British conditions likely to be met. Satisfactory use of any insulating covers (including plastic covered blankets) so far devised makes considerable demands on intelligent planning and on labour for putting them on and taking them off. There are also other disadvantages such as the considerable amount of traffic over the pitch which so far appears to be inseparable from the use of insulating material on the turf. Incidentally, a blanket of snow also provides good insulation!

Fairly small scale trials on pitch protection by means of 'air-houses' (large tents supported by air pressure) carried out in the nineteen sixties showed up various practical difficulties and only one or two big clubs have used them in practice. Air-houses keep off rain, snow and light frosts and can have heat introduced to combat harder frosts. (Heat is also necessary to melt snow as it falls on them to prevent excessive pressure on the fabric.) The cost is such, of course, that the number of organisations which could afford air-houses is very limited.

The same applies to soil-heating to provide unfrozen pitches in frosty weather. Electrical soil warming, pioneered at Bingley over a period of years commencing in 1947, has been installed in a few League soccer pitches, rugby pitches and dog tracks. The system involves the installation of insulated heating cables – typically 150 mm apart, 150 mm deep and providing 108 watts/m² (6 in apart, 6 in deep and providing 10 watts/sq ft) – by means of a machine resembling a mole plough. The cables are fed mains voltage from transformers situated under the stand and in-put is controlled by timeclocks and thermostats.

An alternative form of soil heating, more recently devised, involves forcing warm moist air into pipes installed below the turf and top soil (which has to have special properties), the pipes being perforated in such a manner as to ensure uniform distribution of heat. There is believed to be only one practical installation of this type to date.

From time to time various chemicals are suggested for thawing frozen pitches. So far there are none that can be recommended because they usually damage the grass or the soil and are liable to produce dangerous playing conditions with a chemically-thawed, wet and slippery surface overlying a hard frozen base.

WINTER USE OF GOLF GREENS

For most of the time during the winter months the top soil of the greens is wet and there is very little growth. Under such conditions wear by traffic is most marked.

In the absence of growth the turf tends to become rather thin, thus facilitating invasion by weeds, weed grasses and moss. The moisture in the surface soil acts as a lubricant so that compaction and soil structure damage by traffic is increased.

To counteract this state of affairs much attention needs to be given to drainage in all its aspects. In addition hole changes should be frequent and, as far as practicable, use should be made of the outer regions of the greens. Forking should be carried out as a routine when holes are changed and in some circumstances light applications of sand can be beneficial.

In recent winters there has not been much snow so that the very useful short rest periods that snowfall ensures have been rare. The U.K. rarely experiences long periods of the snowy weather in which prolonged snow cover can lead to turf damage and disease.

Frosty weather is probably the chief enemy to maintaining good greens whilst keeping them in use in winter. Damage caused by play during frosty weather falls into two main categories.

1.   When frozen, plant tissues are easily bruised by players' feet. Following a thaw, browning of the turf can be noted and it is often possible to see footmarks for several weeks, particularly around hole sites. The greater the weight of play in hard frost, obviously the greater becomes the extent of this damage. Areas damaged in this way remain thin for long periods after the frost has disappeared, affecting the trueness of the putting surface well into the growing season. Moreover intensively managed turf affected by frost damage is the more susceptible to fusarium patch disease when milder weather follows.

2.   Long-term damage is caused when play takes place after a sudden thaw. In these conditions the top 12.5 mm (½ in) or so becomes soft whilst the underlying soil remains frozen. Roots are then damaged by a shearing action caused by the players' feet which moves the soft, unfrozen surface across the frozen sub-surface. This creates weak areas which may not recover before the height of the competition season. The surface disturbance is also likely to bring about a marked degree of puddling and disrupt putting surfaces.

238

A good (though not always popular) way to overcome the problem is to provide separate winter greens of, perhaps, 90–180 m² (100–200 sq yd) well clear of the major putting surface, these being finally prepared during the late summer and early autumn and well in advance of when they will be required. Indeed, some work may be required even earlier. Preparation commonly involves mowing down, scarification, top dressing, fertilizer treatment, etc. to produce acceptable putting surfaces. Many clubs do not wish to go to this trouble and quite a number merely site frost holes on the approach. Unfortunately, damage may still be caused by players retrieving balls which go through on to the actual green.

INDEX